V. S. Pritchett

Twayne's English Authors Series

Kinley E. Roby, Editor

Northeastern University

TEAS 445

V. S. PRITCHETT
(1900-   )
Photograph courtesy of Chatto & Windus, London.

V. S. Pritchett

By Dean R. Baldwin

The Behrend College of
The Pennsylvania State University

Twayne Publishers
A Division of G.K. Hall & Co. • *Boston*

V. S. Pritchett
Dean R. Baldwin

Copyright © 1987 by G.K. Hall & Co.
All Rights Reserved
Published by Twayne Publishers
A Division of G.K. Hall & Co.
70 Lincoln Street
Boston, Massachusetts 02111

Copyediting supervised by Lewis DeSimone
Book production by Janet Zietowski
Book design by Barbara Anderson

Typeset in 11 pt. Garamond
by P&M Typesetting, Waterbury, Connecticut

Printed on permanent/durable acid-free paper
and bound in the United States of America

Library of Congress Cataloging in Publication Data

Baldwin, Dean R., 1942–
  V.S. Pritchett.

  (Twayne's English authors series ; TEAS 445)
  Bibliography: p. 125
  Includes index.
  1. Pritchett, V. S. (Victor Sawdon), 1900–   —
Criticism and interpretation. I. Title. II. Title:
VS Pritchett. III. Series.
PR6031.R7Z59   1987   823'.912   86-27121
ISBN 0-8057-6942-0

For my parents

Contents

About the Author

Dean R. Baldwin is assistant professor of English at The Behrend College of The Pennsylvania State University in Erie, where he has been on the faculty since 1975. His undergraduate degree in English and history was awarded by Capital University in Columbus, Ohio, and his graduate degrees in medieval English literature are from Ohio State. He taught at colleges in Missouri and South Dakota before coming to Penn State. He has published in a variety of journals on medieval literature, Shakespeare, modern British fiction, and composition pedagogy. His critical biography of H. E. Bates was published by Susquehanna University Press, and he is currently doing research toward a book on the British short story between the world wars. His research has been supported by the American Philosophical Society, the National Endowment for the Humanities, and Pennsylvania State University. He lives in Erie with his wife and two children.

Preface

In his essay on V. S. Pritchett for the *Dictionary of Literary Biography* Harry S. Marks laments that critics and scholars have ignored the work of V. S. Pritchett to the extent that no biography, bibliography, or extended analysis of his work has yet appeared. This is true in spite of Pritchett's accomplishments in fiction, criticism, and travel writing, and despite the numerous public awards he has received, including a knighthood. As the first detailed examination of Pritchett's life and work, this book begins to fill the needs Marks identified. Specifically, it offers the first objective biography of the author, examines his achievement as a writer of fiction and nonfiction, and begins what I hope will be a reassessment of Pritchett's place in modern British fiction.

Pritchett's most lasting contributions are his short stories. In an age that values the novel above all other literary forms, the short story writer faces some disadvantages in gaining recognition, though there are presently signs of renewed interest in the genre. If so, Pritchett should emerge as a significant figure, not because of any technical innovations but because of his original and skillful use of techniques pioneered by Turgenev, Chekhov, Maupassant, and Dickens, with occasional borrowings from Joyce and Henry James. Pritchett's focus on the seedier aspects of lower middle-class life was influenced primarily by H. G. Wells's novels *Love and Mr. Lewisham, Kipps,* and *The History of Mr. Polly,* and by Arnold Bennett's comic treatments of the same social stratum. Although Pritchett objects to the term, the word *eccentric* is often used to describe his characters, who are usually very odd, though not in outlandish or colorful ways so much as in the notions they have of themselves and the world. Generally, his stories reveal the pretenses, illusions, and misconceptions of these unusual people, though seldom harshly or vindictively. Pritchett's recurring theme is the dignity of the individual and our need for mutual tolerance, forbearance, and understanding. It is not unusual for a reader to begin a Pritchett story by laughing at the characters and to end by sympathizing with them.

Along with his skill of characterization, Pritchett writes with great simplicity, directness, and originality. Wit, clarity, pungency, and incisiveness are the terms his writing calls to mind, for every sentence is deliberate and polished though never self-consciously arty. He has a unique but not idiosyncratic style, lacking any easily describable surface features. Sentences are taut and clear; his vocabulary is simple and direct. He has an uncanny ability to set a scene, usually in a somewhat tattered neighborhood of London, although he is no stranger to the village, the suburb, and the gentleman's club. In the short stories especially, he is a visual artist, word painting not with lush descriptions or piled-up adjectives but with pithy, incisive observations and quick-witted metaphors.

Pritchett's narrative technique in the short stories is equally firm and inventive. Most lack a plot in the conventional sense but are built of trivial events, movements back and forward in time, bits of conversation, glimpses into a character's thoughts, and brief passages of vivid description. From these emerge a pattern and a revelation.

Because there is no extended biography of Pritchett except his own marvelous but highly selective memoirs, I have attempted to uncover as much new information about him as possible. Thus, this book is the first to contain biographical details from Pritchett's private letters with Gerald Brenan, which shed new light on his growth as a writer and on the dramas of his private life. Nonetheless, Pritchett has been successful in keeping most details of his personal life private by granting only occasional press interviews, by remaining outside literary coteries, and by eschewing literary gossip. He is no recluse, having participated for many years in The Society of Authors and P. E. N. (Poets, Essayists, and Novelists), but he is not a public figure. He chooses to reveal only certain facts of his life, and both his many friends and his enemies (if any) have respected his discretion. Biography is crucial to understanding Pritchett's achievements as a writer and the content of much of his fiction. Hence, I have followed an essentially chronological order in discussing his work, with the exception of his nonfiction, which I have reserved for a special chapter at the end. This approach helps to shed light on Pritchett's artistic struggles and on the main themes of his fiction, two of which are particularly important, puritanism, and his obsession (to use his own word) with his father. Over and again, the author's father, Walter Pritchett, appears in novels and stories, usually displaying qualities Pritchett dislikes.

Both as a man and as a writer, Pritchett deserves far more attention than he has received, particularly for his short stories, but also for his novels, criticism, and travel writing. The acclaim that greeted his two retrospective volumes of stories, *Collected Stories* (1982) and *More Collected Stories* (1983), suggests that critics are beginning to recognize the extent of his achievement. Writing of the short story generally, Pritchett once remarked, "[The short story] answers the primitive craving for art, the wit, paradox and beauty of shape, the longing to see a dramatic pattern and significance in our experience, the desire for the electric shock." This is a good description of the pleasure awaiting anyone who reads Pritchett's own finely crafted prose.

I owe much to the encouragement and support of Professor William Peden of the University of Missouri and to Professor Dennis Vannatta of the University of Arkansas, who have generously nurtured my interest in the modern British short story. To the Humanities Research Center of the University of Texas I am indebted for access to the letters and other papers of V. S. Pritchett and Gerald Brenan. My thanks also to Chatto and Windus for their help and cooperation. Special thanks are due to Professor Fred Crawford of the University of Oregon for his many valuable corrections and suggestions, and to Mrs. Norma Hartner, who patiently typed and retyped. Above all, I am grateful for the understanding and encouragement of my wife, Vicki, and our children, Philip and Tanya. Without them, all work would lose its joy.

Dean R. Baldwin

The Behrend College of
The Pennsylvania State University

Chronology

1953 *Books in General;* Christian Gauss Lecturer, Princeton University.

1954 *The Spanish Temper.*

1956 *Collected Stories* (American title, *The Sailor, Sense of Humour and Other Stories*).

1961 *When My Girl Comes Home.*

1962 *London Perceived;* Beckman Professor, University of California, Berkeley.

1963 *Key to My Heart.*

1964 *Foreign Faces* (American title, *Offensive Traveller*).

1965 *New York Proclaimed; The Working Novelist.*

1966 Writer-in-residence, Smith College; *The Saint and Other Stories.*

1968 *A Cab at the Door;* Visiting Professor, Brandeis University.

1969 *Blind Love and Other Stories;* Clark Lecturer, Cambridge; Elected Fellow, Royal Society of Literature; receives C.B.E.

1970 *George Meredith and English Comedy.*

1971 *Midnight Oil;* elected president of English P. E. N.; made Honorary Member of American Academy of Arts and Letters.

1972 Honorary D. Litt. degree, Leeds University.

1973 *Balzac.*

1974 Elected international president of P. E. N., resigns as English president of P. E. N.

1975 Knighted for services to literature.

1976 Ends term as international president of P. E. N.

1977 *The Gentle Barbarian; The Life and Work of Turgenev;* elected president of The Society of Authors.

1978 Resigns as director of the *New Statesman:* Honorary D. Litt. Columbia University.

1979 *The Myth Makers; On the Edge of the Cliff.*

1980 *The Tale Bearers.*

1982 *Collected Stories.*

1983 *More Collected Stories.*

1984 *The Other Side of a Frontier: A V. S. Pritchett Reader.*

1985 *A Man of Letters.*

Chapter One
As Old as the Century

Early Years

Although Victor Sawdon Pritchett always considered himself a Londoner, he was born in the market town of Ipswich, Suffolk, on 16 December 1900. His parents were of the striving lower middle class, his father Walter having been raised in Yorkshire by strict Congregationalists, his mother Beatrice in London by a widow who operated a boarding house. They had met in London where both were employed in a draper's shop, but Walter's ambition was to own his own business, so he brought his bride to Ipswich, where her sister lived, and opened a stationery store. Like virtually all Walter Pritchett's commercial ventures, this one soon failed; accordingly, not long after Victor's birth, Walter returned to London in hopes of finding work. Meanwhile, his young wife took their infant son to Yorkshire to live for a time with her in-laws. Throughout his childhood Pritchett moved many times, on some occasions spending months with relatives in Yorkshire or Ipswich, otherwise moving with his family from one London suburb to another. As a result, he grew up in both city and country, and his writing manifests this division: in his early years he was driven by a passion for natural description, while his mature works focus on urban settings and characters.[1]

Victor remained an only child for less than two years. His brother Cyril was born 15 July 1902, and a second brother, Gordon, was born in 1910. Between these two brothers was a sister, Kathleen, born 20 September 1906, whom he never mentions by name.[2] Life in these early years for the Pritchett children was unstable, unpredictable, even fantastic. Their father's mercurial nature led him to jump from one job to another, usually as a traveling salesman. Since he always spent more money than he earned, the family flitted from house to house when not taking refuge with relatives in Yorkshire or Ipswich. By age twelve Victor had lived in a dozen or more houses and dingy flats. "Before too long in one place, the cabbie and his horse would be coughing at the door; a drive to the Underground, a new home in any of the interchangeable suburbs, Palmers Green, Balham, Uxbridge, Acton, Ealing, Hammersmith, Camberwell, Woodford, Dulwich, Bromley."[3] These frequent moves destroyed any sense of permanence or continuity in the family's life and made shambles of the children's education, but they were hardest on Pritchett's mother. Flighty and impetuous, she suffered from Walter's instability, the responsibilities of four young children, isolation, and poverty. She made matters worse by her own slapdash nature, as when she impulsively attacked the velvet window curtains to make the boys trousers, which, because of her shoddy sewing, came apart at the seams. On one occasion Victor was about to win the two-hundred-yard dash when his shorts fell down, spoiling his only chance at a school sports ribbon. As the family's fortunes declined, she became increasingly unkempt, her hair falling about her face, her blouse undone, her apron rough and unclean. She was not a good cook.

Walter, by contrast, was elegantly dressed, scrupulously clean, and very well fed. He was unconsciously selfish and egotistical, denying his family everything and himself nothing. While spending lavishly on his own clothes and accessories, he did not notice that his wife was always short of money and his children were becoming guttersnipes. As a traveling salesman for a succession of companies, he stayed in good hotels, ate lavish meals, and treated himself to first-class train fare and Christmas pantomimes, while his family lived on what was left. He returned on weekends like a petty prince, sometimes with a present of fish or meat, but always with a remarkable and largely imaginary story of his sales and importance. His family's job was to provide an appreciative audience and treat him regally. Mother knelt and removed his shoes and socks; he sat in the best chair, ate the best cut of meat, and lived in comparative glamour and complete freedom while denying the slightest independence to his wife and children. They existed to do his will and any sign of rebellion produced in him not violence or wrath but uncomprehending pain. A solipsist and dreamer, he lived in a world of his own where, like the wealthy entrepreneurs he envied, he was energetic and far-seeing, shrewd and inventive. Victor Pritchett always remembered two incidents as epitomizing his father. Behind the house in Uxbridge ran a canal, which Walter Pritchett imagined to be an important river. He bought a blazer, yachting cap, cream trousers, and a monocle. While old men fished in the dirty water, he strolled up and down pretentiously, dreaming he was among yachtsmen. The second occurred at the house in Ealing, which had a tiny ornamental balcony. To Walter, the balcony was the perfect place to eat breakfast—as if part of a villa overlooking the Riviera.

By the time Victor was ten, his father's frequent and prolonged absences from home and his mother's increasing vagueness left him and his brother Cyril free to run the streets of London. According to Pritchett's memoirs, they became rowdy, dirty, ill-mannered urchins. Pritchett perhaps exaggerates, but Camberwell then (as now) was a rough neighborhood. Their flat on a street just off Coldharbour Lane sat next to a mechanized bakery and vibrated day and night to the clatter of its machinery. Beside the bakery was a roller rink, thrumming with the rumble of skates and thumping to the beat of a band. Victor and Cyril attended St. Matthew's school, where the pupils sat in rows of benches and teachers kept an uneasy peace with the cane. Irregular schooling had made Victor an indifferent student, but at St. Matthews he excelled at shorthand which he later called his first encounter with a foreign language. The health inspector removed lice from dirty heads; ragtime emanated from forbidden picture houses; a new Jack the Ripper terrorized the streets and made Victor fear for five-year-old Kathleen, whom he collected every day after school. In the mysterious adult world of home the boys were kept awake at night by endless quarrels over "That woman," who turned out to be not Walter's mistress (he was not a philanderer), but Mary Baker Eddy. Walter had run the gamut of dissenting Protestantism and settled in the mind-over-matter world of Christian Science.

The vagaries of the family fortunes often separated Victor and Cyril from their parents and each other during the summer months, Victor going to Yorkshire, Cyril to Ipswich. The crash of 1910, however, was more serious than previous setbacks, for this time everyone except Walter went to Ipswich. Supported by Uncle Bugg, the family took a small house on Clifford Road at the edge of town. It was a completely different world from the urban chaos of London. Uncle Bugg and his family were staunch Presbyterians, solid middle-class citizens of sober respectability, comfortable and commonsensical.

The Ipswich period was a pleasant interlude for Victor, especially because his father was absent. Cyril worshiped Walter and wanted above all to be noticed by him, but Victor was happiest when he was away. There were other pleasures as well. The family, minus father, was together and at peace, and Ipswich offered a wider freedom than London, with the countryside not far away. Victor and Cyril sat in a favorite chestnut tree, smoking shreds of old window blinds rolled into crude cigarettes or stuffed into elderberry pipes. Life was freer and its tone was higher. Uncle Bugg occasionally took the boys to see his construction company in action, and once they went to Felixstowe for their first glimpse of the sea. Aunt Ada affected a lorgnette and an interest in art, with the result that Victor's earliest ambition was to become a painter in the manner of the watercolorist Barlow Woods. Painting appealed to him as an entrance to another world, one without strife or arguments.

The Ipswich interlude lasted only a year, for in the interim Walter Pritchett had indeed improved the family finances and was once again relatively prosperous. He brought his wife and children to a substantial villa in Dulwich, at 200 Clive Road. Nearby were Alleyn's School, Dulwich College, and the Horniman Museum.[4] They arrived from Ipswich in May but were not enrolled in school for the remainder of that year nor when school reopened in the fall. As usual, Walter was in no hurry to look after their education, perhaps because it encouraged independence. It also involved acting on a decision, and Walter Pritchett preferred evasions and idle scheming to anything definite, so prospectuses of public schools were sent for and dawdled over. Victor began to imagine himself at a public school, wearing a cap and blazer, but Walter delayed so long that Beatrice, in desperation, finally walked the boys to Rosendale Junior School and enrolled them there. It was already mid-October 1911.[5] Characteristically, Walter had neglected to provide even clothing money for the boys, so mother plundered his wardrobe, recklessly cutting down two pairs of his trousers and tacking the seams so carelessly that at recess the Pritchett boys stood immobilized while the other children played. Rosendale was a typical school of its time; its major failing from Victor's point of view was its emphasis on rote learning and iron discipline, which broke the children's spirits without engaging their intellects or imaginations. Luckily, Victor escaped some of this sternness, for his first teacher at Rosendale was W. W. Bartlett, who was progressive in his methods and given a free hand by the headmaster. He freed his pupils from dreary recitation and the usual textbooks to involve them in group activities, drawing, and poetry—not the dead literature of previous centuries, but new poems by living authors from the *English Review*. Discipline was enforced by a punishment worse than the cane—letters of apology to Mr. Bartlett that had to be perfect in every respect. He awakened young Victor's imagination.

Bartlett also encouraged Pritchett's early reading. What money he could cadge from his mother was spent on The Penny Poets, *Paradise Regained,* Wordsworth, and others. These he would take to a little "summer house" in the back garden, a sort of shed with a stained-glass window where he could sit inside or on the roof and read in comparative peace.[6] When money gave out, he crept into his father's "study," where unread business magazines lay on the tables and leather-bound editions of Marcus Aurelius, Marie Corelli, and Shakespeare competed with Hall Caine and something called *In Tune with the Infinite.* A Christmas gift of *Oliver Twist* put him into "hot terror" because what it described seemed so familiar and real; a friend introduced him to H. G. Wells. Boys' magazines like the *Gem* and the *Magnet* filled the need for lighter, more exciting fare until Walter discovered them and forbade his son to bring such trash into the house. One of Mr. Bartlett's classroom projects was a literary magazine for which Victor wrote sixty or seventy lines in imitation of Coleridge's "Christabel." A classmate tore its feeble images to shreds, and even the kindly Bartlett disapproved. Defeated, Victor turned to prose and tried a novel on an exotic Moorish subject, full of battles and laments. Again his efforts brought humiliation: parts of this work were read aloud to the family and ridiculed by father. The ordeal ended with one of Walter's lectures on a businessman's hopes for his sons and with young Victor conceiving more bitter hatred than ever toward his father.

Walter Pritchett thought of himself in especially grandiose terms during this period because he was momentarily successful. Capitalizing on the Edwardian mania for fancy upholstery, he had established a factory for making chair covers, tea cozies, and the like—with capital put up by someone else, of course. Pritchett's partner and the secretary of the firm was a young and attractive woman, Miss H, as she is called in Pritchett's autobiography. According to Walter, God ran the business and "right ideas" were more important than capital or profit. Still, he left the house early each morning to make certain that the workers did not arrive late or waste company time, though no one did less work than he.

Meanwhile, Victor's schooling went ahead unevenly. The headmaster judged Mr. Bartlett's experimental methods unsound after one year. Victor's second teacher at Rosendale was a young woman of disturbing figure and good looks who did what she could to undo the supposed damage of Bartlett's forays into self-expression and the modern arts, reinstating rote memorization and the cane. However, she did kindle one flame. Shortly before a holiday she offered a prize to the student who produced the best drawing over the break. Victor found his subject in Horniman's Museum, Indian amulets, which he copied and colored. Since most of the other children forgot the competition, Victor won—the only prize of his school career. He asked for books by Ruskin, and a few weeks later was presented with eight volumes of art and literary criticism. This momentary success led to thoughts of further triumphs, and Victor was taken to Streatham to sit for a scholarship. Here the irregularities of his schooling and the innovations of Mr. Bartlett proved devastating. The questions baffled him, except one on Noah and the flood, which inspired a wild fiction, full of the laments of the drowning. He was not surprised to learn he had failed. So he stayed at Rosendale school, nursing his ambition to become a writer, confused and appalled by the older boys' talk of sex, entertained by attending movies against his father's orders. As if to compensate for arriving late at Rosendale, he stayed until he was overage, remaining until August 1914. School records show that he earned marks of "four" on a scale of one to five, but no one today knows whether five was the top score or the bottom. He may have been below average or above.[7]

After the summer holidays many of Victor's friends were apprenticed in trades or took full-time jobs, but the Pritchett family business was still prospering, so Victor and Cyril were enrolled in Alleyn's grammar school. It was several steps below a public school, and most of the boys were from homes like the Pritchetts' where aspirations were relatively low. Typically they became junior clerks in banks and offices, part of the lower echelons of the British middle classes. Nevertheless, the curriculum included French and German, and in these languages Victor discovered his true talent. While his marks in English, science, and mathematics were average, he did very well in foreign languages, a liberating discovery about himself that was to shape his future profoundly. Still, this was not a good time to be in school, for World War I had erupted when Victor left Rosendale. Not long after he entered Alleyn's, the regular faculty began leaving for the front, to be replaced by aged teachers called out of retirement. At Alleyn's as elsewhere, these superannuated masters were often the butt of cruel jokes, for they lacked the authority to teach or discipline, and their approach was rigidly traditional. The combined discouragements of an inept faculty and a curriculum that excluded art made Victor's experience at Alleyn's rather dull and dreary, though there were some moments of success. On one occasion the boys' excited and bloodthirsty talk about an air raid on London prompted one of the English masters to assign an essay on bombings. Victor puzzled over the problem for some time before hitting on the novelist's solution. Taking the point of view of his terrified mother, he produced something more like a story than an essay and dubiously handed it in. When it was read aloud in class, he cowered in fear, convinced that it would be ridiculed; instead, he found he had again produced a triumph. Once more he was proclaimed a genius for a few weeks, but his next attempt—this time a description of his reactions to classical music—failed miserably.

The war also changed the Pritchetts' home life. Walter interpreted the outbreak of hostilities as a sign that he should enlarge the business, so he took new premises and outfitted the showroom with new display cases. The boys were taken to admire the remodeling, but the impression left by the visit was not of the new factory or its fixtures but of their father's relationship to these. For the first time they realized that here was their father's real home. What he owned in the factory, the authority he wielded in the shop, the trappings and fixtures he bought for his office and showrooms were more authentically domestic and important to him than anything at home. There is no doubt that Victor resented being relegated to second place in his father's affections, just as he came to despise the materialism of his aspirations. A change in factory locations suggested a change in homes also, so the family moved from the house in Dulwich, the only one that had ever seemed like home. The new house was a villa in Bromley, then on the edge of London. An additional shock came when Walter was ordered to work in an aircraft factory at a wage of two pounds a week. From managing director of his own firm he descended to mere clerk, and the factory was not in London but in Hertfordshire. Miss H was left to run the upholstery business and probably fared better without her partner. Victor could breathe more easily now that father came home only occasionally. Nevertheless, it was during this period that one of the few moments of intimacy occurred between them. Hurrying to cadet drill at school, Victor tripped and severely sprained his ankle. For the first time his father explained the principles of Christian Science and its doctrines regarding evil and disease. He encouraged Victor to think of his injury as an error in perception that could be cured by believing that nothing bad could exist in God's kingdom. Victor tried to believe and for several days hobbled painfully on his foot until, as father had predicted, it healed. He began reading the *Christian Science Monitor* and tried to comprehend Mrs. Eddy's book. For the time being, at least, he was converted.

The years 1914–16 were crucial to everything that followed. At Allyn's he discovered his ability in languages, but the most important events were occurring outside school, in the battles of home life and in the spiritual and intellectual strife he encountered as a Christian Scientist. At the time, young Victor strove to accept his father's faith, perhaps to appease the man he so often opposed and hated. But in retrospect he acknowledged that part of his motivation for attending services was a desire to make new friends. His father had always prohibited anyone from visiting the house and resented bitterly his sons' natural desire to mix with others their age. The Pritchett children, like their mother, felt prisoners in their own home. The attractions of Sunday School, therefore, with some pretty girls attending and a fleshy, middle-aged teacher with melony breasts only barely concealed by a plunging neckline, were irresistible. Still, the faith offered less sensual attractions: it appealed to a youth's idealism, and it set the Pritchetts apart from their neighbors, an attitude their father encouraged.

But for all its attractions, practical and ideal, the faith ran counter to two deep instincts. First, official church doctrine discouraged interest in the arts because they appealed to the senses. Like caffeine and alcohol, art was something to renounce in the name of religion, a practice that Victor naturally found inimical to his creative inclinations. The other problem was sex, for Victorian self-denial was still influential among Christian Scientists. With a youthful body that betrayed him into erections at the mere sight of an attractive girl and a mind that was taught to repress the urgings of his body, Victor was torn between a chaste ideal and physical reality. These conflicts affected him deeply. Chastity was a badge that he wore proudly into his twenties, and guilt over sexuality persisted into his middle years. He often remarked that he did not know passion until he married Dorothy, and when we consider that this was in 1936, the depth of the problem becomes apparent. What is true of the man is true of the artist. It is difficult to find in Pritchett's fiction any character, male or female, who is emotionally fulfilled or sexually well adjusted. Nor is there a character for whom sex is rewarding until the *Camberwell Beauty* in 1974.

During his years in Alleyn's School Victor appeared to others as a fairly bright, clean-cut, promising boy with a flair for languages and an interest in writing and art. Inside he was a turmoil of repressed and conflicting desires. Evidence of his growing facility in French came one afternoon as he found himself reading Moliere's *L'Avare* with pleasure and understanding, while proficiency in German was shown by his translating a Christian Science tract into English. The chaos of his home life was alleviated by his father's frequent absences, while the future held at least the possibility of university—not Oxford or Cambridge, of course, but perhaps one of the red-bricks, assuming that he was not drafted as cannon fodder for the western front. At least he felt safe in assuming that he would complete grammar school before facing any difficult decisions about his future. These comfortable assumptions were upset by a visit from his paternal grandfather, a minister for whom education had meant liberation from a life in the army or as a fisherman. Unaccountably, grandfather suggested that young Victor be sent to work, and Walter, never enthusiastic about education, abruptly and promptly removed him from school only weeks before his sixteenth birthday. All his hopes, he thought, were crushed. There would be no French prize at school, no diploma, no chance for university. Instead, he suddenly found himself an apprentice in the leather trade. He felt betrayed; his ambition to write was being snatched away with his last opportunity at education.

The firm to which he was apprenticed had its offices on Weston Street in Bermondsey, the traditional center of London's leather trade on the south bank of the Thames, midway between London and Tower Bridges and not far from Chaucer's Tabbard Inn. His father had encouraged him during the nervous first journey to this factory to adopt the attitude young Samuel had taken when hearing the voice of God: "Speak, Lord, thy servant heareth." It was perhaps the only good advice Walter ever gave his son, for the owner was a Dickensian figure who ran his company with an iron hand. Victor's position was that of junior clerk, and his duties were to wait on customers, copy letters, and carry messages about London. These he found easier than school work, but the hours were long, from nine in the morning to seven in the evening on weekdays, and Saturdays until mid-afternoon. In many ways the bright spot of his week was still the Sunday School hour when he could mix with young people, especially girls. Nevertheless, the job had its compensations. After a short period of being intimidated by inner London's noise and dirt, Pritchett began to find adventure in the city:

It was disagreeable at first to be put into the malodorous leather trade, but the animality of skins fascinated me and so did the Bermondsey leather dressers and fellmongers. The smell of that London of my boyhood and bowler-hatted youth is still with me. I coughed my way through a city stinking, rather excitingly, of coal smoke, gas escapes, tanyards, breweries, horse manure and urine. Flies swarmed, people scratched their fleas. The streets smelled of beer; men and boys reeked of hair oil, Vaseline, strong tobacco, powerful boot polish, mackintoshes and things like my father's voluptuous cachous.[8]

The city had other attractions, too. Errands could be lengthened into explorations, and lunch hours could be used for browsing in bookshops, walking to places as far away as Fleet Street, or listening to organ concerts in nearby churches. The Thames and its traffic were only a few blocks away. The office itself was staffed by individualists interesting enough to be turned later into fiction, among them two female clerks who stimulated Victor's erotic imagination and provoked suggestive remarks from the men. For a time these attractions were enough, but eventually the routine palled and the jokes became stale. From sheer frustration he picked a fight with the retarded boy who did menial jobs. Fortunately, the proprietor recognized the problem and, instead of firing him, moved Victor to the warehouse where he could learn the trade in earnest.

In his new assignment Victor was put under one of the owner's four sons and set to the task of learning to judge and grade hides. It was good training for a writer, exercising his powers of observation and requiring that he describe consignments accurately and succinctly. By the end of his time with the firm he could identify hides not only as to animal but also as to which of England's numerous country tanneries had prepared them. This was far more interesting and varied work than the dull routine of the office. It also enabled him to meet many tannery owners, and for a time his enthusiasm for the business was so great that he aspired to become a tanner himself. During his second summer with the firm he took a cycling holiday to Ipswich and along the way called on a country tanner. Showing off before his pretty daughter, he fell into one of the curing tanks and had to be fished out of the stinking liquid, mortified. Eventually, however, his interest in the business declined, ironically because of the people he met. Literary culture was common then, and various older members of the firm and even some visitors introduced him to authors he had not read, especially modern ones like Robert Louis Stevenson, Hilaire

Belloc, and Arnold Bennett. The varying opinions of those he met also reawakened his interest in literary criticism. As he had sometimes done while at Alleyn's school, he began spending lunch money on books, and his ambition to become a writer revived and grew stronger as the years passed. By 1918 he was beginning to weary of the trade and the dead-end life it offered, but there was a war in progress, and Victor was becoming old enough to fight in it. Vaguely, he thought of entering the air corps.

The armistice signed only a few weeks before Victor's eighteenth birthday ended idle speculation about the air corps and suggested new possibilities for the future. It also brought Walter home from his wartime job in Hertfordshire. The experience there had changed him, and not for the better. Having seen business run on a large scale, he was more dissatisfied than ever with the modest success of the upholstery company, and he became impatient for newer and ever larger premises. Frustrated in this by Miss H, he went on a buying spree, purchasing furniture, clothes, silverware, and—to Cyril's delight—a Sunbeam car. At the time Cyril wanted to become an auto mechanic, but Walter forbade any such sign of independence, and so Cyril secretly took a job in a garage. Sneaking around was the only way the boys could pursue their ambitions: Victor became adept at lying so he could write, see his girl friend, or attend an extension course at night. Here lightning struck the third time when his essay on Milton was praised by the lecturer as the work of a professional writer. This success, like the ones before it, conferred new status, and he was allowed to attend the lectures without lying. He began seeking out people interested in literature and found a good friend two doors away, a young French pianist who was a musical prodigy. It was good to discover another young man to whom art was important, a friend equally contemptuous of suburban aspirations and bourgeois values. He encouraged Victor's desire to leave home and begin his own life. Through all this, Walter was becoming increasingly difficult and dictatorial, as he could not face the inevitable letting go. Victor suffered less than Cyril, whom constant bullying had long since made a stammerer at home, though not outside it. After leaving school, he had tried for months to persuade Walter to take him into the business or let him get a job, but to no avail. Finally, on his own initiative, he found a position with an excellent French company dealing in textiles and went off to Lyons to learn the trade. Eventually, he made an excellent living in the business, but, what is more important, his flight was an inspiration to Victor. It was possible to escape and survive.

For the present, however, Victor was stuck in the leather trade. His essay on Milton made the rounds of literary magazines and was rejected by them all. If his best effort was not good enough to publish, what hope was there for him to succeed as a writer? Then, almost providentially, he was struck by the postwar Spanish influenza, so seriously that Walter abandoned his principles and sent for a doctor. It was a long illness and a slow recovery, but as so often happens, it signaled a change. A bonus from the company of ten pounds, plus his own savings, gave him a total of twenty pounds, a pitifully small sum, but all he needed. He turned his back on London and the leather trade and took his money, his ambition, his fears, and his father's warnings and set his eyes resolutely on Paris. He would be independent or return in disgrace. At twenty, Victor Sawdon Pritchett left the leather trade and set out to make himself a writer.

Paris and After

Fortunately for a young man with only high school French and no experience of foreign travel, Victor was met at the Gare du Nord by a friend of Walter's, a Mr. Hotchkiss, who showed the young man about the city until Victor realized he must find a very cheap hotel and begin looking for work. There was a tiny Christian Science congregation in Paris, ministering to English and American tourists and a few French converts, but none of them was able to provide a job. At the end of three weeks the twenty pounds had almost disappeared, but Victor answered a newspaper advertisement and was hired as a clerk in the Paris branch of a British photography supply house and given the job of checking orders in and out, writing letters, and eventually waiting on customers. At first his spoken French was laughably bad, prompting friends to suggest a "sleeping dictionary" as the best way to learn the language, but like the young man in "The Diver," he was proud of his chastity and took offense at the suggestion. His virginity was the office joke, and his fellow workers often "auctioned" him in the streets to female passers-by. He was paid less than the 18/6 he had earned at the leather factory, and so it was all he could do to afford a cheap room in the Auteuil and buy meals. Still, he had declared his independence and won.[9]

Having secured the essentials, he turned to the problem of becoming a writer but had no idea of how to begin. Had he been more alert, he might have joined the growing cadre of artists and writers assembling in Paris during the early 1920s, but he was unaware of their presence and indeed of the whole avant-garde movement. Thus, for a time he imitated Stevenson and Belloc and simply walked, first all over Paris, then outside it, miles and miles at weekends. Nothing happened. Then he remembered the only practical advice he had ever read, a discussion in J. M. Barrie's *When a Man's Single* in which an experienced journalist advises an aspiring writer to forget about airing his lofty political or philosophical ideas and to concentrate on what was under his nose. "They [aspiring authors] should write of the things they have seen. Newspaper readers have an insatiable appetite for knowing how that part of the world lives with which they are not familiar. They want to know how the Norwegians cook their dinners and build their houses, and ask each other in marriage."[10] Later in the conversation the journalist gives examples of how the most commonplace items and events have served as the basis for lively articles. It was excellent advice, but there was a part of it that Pritchett either had forgotten or could not believe—that successful writers do not have to be well read. Feeling that he needed to complete his literary education, he plowed determinedly through as many French, English, and Russian authors as he could, becoming increasingly discouraged because the task was endless. Perhaps he was simply stalling for time, trying to work up the courage to begin. Finally, Barrie's advice prevailed and he forced himself to write a description of his first room in Paris and the night sounds of the neighborhood. He typed the results and sent them along with two more articles to the *Saturday Westminster, Time and Tide,* and the *Christian Science Monitor.* In a few months responses came back from all three: the articles had been accepted. He could write.

A young man alone in Paris, even a chaste one intent on becoming a writer, must sooner or later fall under the spell of a girl. In Pritchett's case she was Judy Lang, daughter of a young and pretty widow lately arrived from Mexico to await compensation for losing an estate there. They met at a Christian Science service, and before long Victor was considered by Judy's student friends to be her lover. In fact, they spent their time in innocent walks along the Seine or through the parks, for Judy was more doll than woman and was separated from Victor by class and breeding. Mrs. Lang's expected money never did materialize, and so she was forced into a succession of posts as a governess, while Judy babysat small children. The ten pounds that Vic-

tor had earned by writing was soon wheedled out of him by the artful
Mrs. Lang and never repaid. Years later, however, when Pritchett
needed a novella to complete his first collection of stories, he transformed Mrs. Lang into Mrs. Lance, moved the action to Spain, and
called the result "The Spanish Virgin" (1930). The story was not a
success, but at least he recovered his ten pounds.

By the time he met Mrs. Lang and her daughter, Victor had been
in Paris for about a year. He had mastered French on two levels, the
formal and the colloquial, and he had met a variety of interesting people, among them a Mr. Shaves, who worked in a bank but aspired to
act. He introduced Pritchett to two businessmen who offered him, at
twice his clerk's salary, a job selling glue and shellac. It was agreeable
work, for it took him out of the office and into dozens of little shops
all over Paris. Unfortuntely for his employers, Pritchett was more adept at engaging customers in literary discussions than in selling his
wares. After several months of no success, he was given a last chance
with a consignment of ostrich feathers, but they had gone out of fashion and he made no sales. He was given a month's severance pay and
fired. After eighteen months of steady work, he felt liberated by
money in his pocket and time on his hands. He saw it as an opportunity for sexual adventure and attempted to prepare by trying to buy
some condoms. Guilt and fear made him so nervous that he could
not tell the pharmacist what he wanted, so the clerk finally wrapped
something in paper and slid it across the counter. Victor ran out with
the package and put it, unopened, into a drawer in his room. So
much for sexual adventure.

Losing his job was not immediately a blow because he was writing
quite regularly for British magazines and had even been commissioned by the *Monitor* to do a series of ten illustrated articles. All but
two of these were severely cut, but he nevertheless felt justified by
the commission in calling himself a professional writer. At about this
time he also began seeing a friend of Judy's, a Danish philosophy student working on her dissertation. Tall, bony, and critical of Victor's
writing, she seemed paradoxically indifferent toward him and jealous
of his supposed relationship with Judy. Much to his pain, she forced
him one day to confess his virginity, whereupon he blurted out that
he would like to sleep with her. Ashamed, he literally ran away and
avoided her for the next few days until she slipped a note under his
door, asking to see him again. They met and returned to his room.
After the usual fumbling with buttons and hooks, Victor went into

the next room, opened his secret package, and found not condoms but liver pills! In his panic he took two, tried to explain to the girl, and lost himself in her arms. Later, as they walked along the Seine, the significance of what he had been trying to say dawned on her. She laughed helplessly for hours.

Although he was regularly selling short articles and sketches, Pritchett was running precariously low on money. Then, disaster struck. The *Christian Science Monitor* became caught in a squabble between two factions of the church and was unable to pay for Victor's articles. Money became so short that he sold his books and his best suit; when that money had gone, he sought out Percy, a "saintly bore" who on an earlier occasion had subjected Victor to an afternoon of tedious séances, an episode he later fictionalized in *Dead Man Leading*. Percy would lend money to anyone, but when this "loan" was spent, Victor was too ashamed to beg for more and was on the verge of starving when his landlady sternly took him in her motherly hands, fed him a good bowl of soup, and lent him five francs. After more lean days and a pathetic return to Christian Science services in hopes of being invited for a meal, he received a check for fifteen pounds from a church member who was upset that he had not been paid for his articles. He repaid his debts and shortly thereafter found a job selling theater tickets. Once more he failed. By this time Paris was losing its charm. After two years of surviving on his own, he grew tired of the city and returned to London.

Back in his own country, Pritchett quickly discovered that his modest achievements in Paris were insufficient to qualify him for a job with any of the literary magazines in London. Once again, however, Christian Scientists were willing to take a chance. With no relevant experience and no understanding of politics, he was commissioned to write a series of eight articles on Ireland, which had recently won Home Rule and was now fighting a civil war. In January of 1923 he left for Dublin, so innocent of its politics that he unknowingly arrived looking exactly like an IRA gunman. Some friends took away his dangerous clothes and installed him in a temperance hotel.[11] From Dublin he traveled westward by stages to Cork, Limerick, and Enniskillen, where he met a traveling salesman whose habit of giving his girlfriend rides in his father's hearse would later result in one of his finest stories, "A Sense of Humour." But that was far in the future. At the moment he had only sketchy and essentially touristy information on which to base his articles, but he wrote four and sent them in, assuming the worst. To his surprise, they were accepted, and he was given a regular job. For the next year he sent articles on the Irish "troubles" to the *Monitor,* signing them VSP. These duties being hardly burdensome, he had ample time for traveling into the countryside, browsing in bookshops, attending the Abbey Theatre, and even spending a weekend at a country estate, an experience that would later become part of his first novel, *Clare Drummer* (1929). Pritchett had walked the streets of Paris, oblivious to the literary revolution in progress all around him; in Dublin he was a little better informed. He took lunch with James Stephens, paid a respectful visit to Yeats, and called on Sean O'Casey. After a year he was suddenly called back to London and assumed he would be fired. Instead, he was taken to lunch, told that readers were tired of Ireland, and asked if he would like to go to Spain with a salary of four hundred pounds a year. Knowing not a word of Spanish and as ignorant of Spain as he had been of Ireland, he agreed.

Alert readers of Pritchett's autobiography might note that chapter 6 of *Midnight Oil* begins, "At the beginning of January in 1924, shortly after my twenty-third birthday, we set off for Madrid" (139). This sudden shift from "I" to "we" is explained by the fact that during his year in Ireland, Pritchett had met and married Evelyn Maude Vigors in a civil ceremony on 3 January 1924.[12] Virtually nothing is known about Pritchett's wife except that she was an actress and that she remained married to Pritchett until 1936. How they met, when they courted, how they fared during their marriage, and why they divorced are unknown except to themselves. The reference quoted above is one of the few times Pritchett mentions his first marriage. Even in the extensive correspondence with Gerald Brenan, he remarks on it only once or twice, calling the marriage "disastrous." The opening pages of Pritchett's first published book, *Marching Spain* (1928), allude to an unnamed woman unhappy about his leaving her to gather the material for the book; and it seems likely that a partial portrait of Evelyn is given in the heroine of *Clare Drummer,* but there is only a bare hint in one letter to A. D. Peters to justify this. Pritchett's extreme reticence about the marriage indicates a painful experience, but apart from one or two suggestions of sexual incompatibility in his letters, he gives no hints about the nature of their relationship or their reasons for divorce.

If Pritchett's departure for France in 1920 had marked a break with his father-dominated youth, then the move to Spain was to provide an equally important "moral shock." The soft, romantic scenery of Yorkshire and Suffolk, together with the dissolving mists of Ireland, had helped produce something Wordsworthian in his character and sensibility. The harsh, barren landscape of northern Spain gradually wrought a change in perspective that ultimately ran very deep. In his own words, "There was a sense of the immediate and finite, so much more satisfying than the infinite, which had really starved me; a sense of the physical not of the spiritual. I felt I was human" (MO, 143). This change was hardly instantaneous, nor was it the product simply of landscape and climate. Settling in Madrid, Pritchett and Evelyn learned Spanish from the German woman who was their first land-lady, and as their command of the language improved, they began moving in the advanced and agnostic circles of the city, with students, poets, professors at Madrid University, and other journalists. For Pritchett, with a male's freedom in Spain, this was a time of rapid and important growth, equivalent to what many of his contemporaries experienced in the cafés of Paris. His mind became sharper as he struggled through Croce in Spanish and listened to the philosophical, religious, and political debates of his new friends. For Evelyn, however, it must have been far less invigorating, for she returned to Ireland for long periods during the two years that Victor worked in Spain. Two authors were also important to his development: Unamuno, whose *Del sentimento trágico de la vida* emphasized the intensity of life in the face of death, and Pio Barojo, whose novels burned with pessimism, atheism, and sympathy for his characters. Between them, they helped to scorch away the "diluted transcendentalism" of Pritchett's religious instruction.

Journalism made no great demands on his time, so with a passion for travel, Pritchett set out by foot, train, bus, or car to see "the Spains." During the two years he spent as the *Monitor's* correspondent, he traveled extensively, forming a lifelong attachment to the country that would result in two books and numerous visits, plus the friendship of his acknowledged master in Spanish studies, Gerald Brenan.

In spite of the rather good salary, the opportunities for travel, and the chances to meet interesting people from all walks of life, after two years he began to tire of journalism. Having no real interest in politics and no special aptitude for reporting, he was finding the work dull and unrewarding. His passion simply to write and be published was giving way to a desire to write fiction. His problem was to find a suitable subject. At last, seizing on the report of a gypsy quarrel, he labored over the problems of character and dialogue and in 1923 wrote his first story, "Rain in the Sierra." It was not published for three years, nor is it very accomplished, for though it swells with vivid, sharp descriptions, its ironies are heavy-handed, its characters shallow, and its psychology dubious. Nevertheless, it was a beginning.

After Pritchett had been in Spain for nearly two years, the volatile politics of the country settled into dull stability, eliminating the need for a special correspondent. Pritchett, therefore, was dispatched to Morocco to cover the Riff rebellion, and from there went to Algiers, Constantine, Tunisia, and finally the United States. Boston (home of Christian Science) bored him, so he traveled to the logging country of Quebec and afterward embarked on a long hike down the spine of the Appalachians as far as South Carolina, filling notebooks with transcriptions of Southern dialect and purple passages of description. By late 1925 or early 1926 his career had come full circle and he found himself once again in Dublin. There he wrote more short stories: "Tragedy in a Greek Theatre," "The White Rabbit," "Night in a Corsican Inn," and "The Mad Feller." At last the *Monitor*'s patience with his reporting grew thin, and in 1927 he was fired. Returning to London, he felt defeated, as if seven years of independence in several countries on three continents had resulted in nothing except a few stories and reams of journalistic hackwork. Occupying cheap rooms in Charlotte Street, he and Evelyn (who had enjoyed some success as an actress in the Abbey Theatre and was now with a small London repertory company) struggled to survive. Pritchett tried all the newspapers that advertised for reporters and pestered editors of literary magazines, but the only work he could find was translating Spanish business letters. Finally the pressure to write drove him to desperate measures: in the spring of 1927 he left again for Spain, determined to gather materials for a book. He was away nearly three months, walking from Badajoz to Leon along a route taken by Wellington during the Peninsular War (1809–1813). When he returned and began writing of his frantic trek, he did so from a series of cheap London rooms, as if his father's restless spirit were driving him. He had enough business sense, however, to engage the services of literary agent A. D. Peters, and the decision paid off immediately. Ernest Benn, a small London publisher, accepted the book, called *Marching Spain*, and paid an advance of twenty-five pounds. Two chapters were also sold to *Travel Magazine* in America for twenty pounds. [13]

Pritchett's return to London in 1927 marked the beginning of a difficult transition from journalist to free-lance writer. To survive, he had to supplement what little he could earn by writing fiction or travel articles with literary journalism. Again, the *Christian Science Monitor* lent a hand, this time by making him book review editor and requiring him to write a weekly review of his own. He augmented the five pounds a week he derived from this by occasional reviews for the *New Statesman* and other periodicals. During 1928 he published three short stories—"Fishy" (*Manchester Guardian,* 9 February), "Sack of Lights" (*Outlook,* 10 March), and "In the Haunted Room" (*New Statesman,* 24 March)—but even in 1928 a beginning writer could not earn his livelihood or establish a reputation solely through short stories, and so Pritchett spent much of 1928 and 1929 writing his first novel, *Clare Drummer.* His advance was the princely sum of seventy-five pounds, the publisher again being Benn (Ernest Benn to ADP, 7 June 1929). Thus, in two years he had managed to effect the change from full-time journalist to free-lance writer, and the rhythm of his working life had essentially been established. He would support himself primarily by literary journalism—as many book reviews, essays, and travel articles as he could write, but his real life as a writer would begin after business hours, when he would turn to short stories and novels.

In hindsight, 1930 would appear an ideal time to launch a literary career in Britain. The old guard, dominated by Arnold Bennett, John Galsworthy, Joseph Conrad, the Powys brothers, Ford Madox Ford, and Somerset Maugham, was fading away, and a new generation of writers, inspired by James Joyce and T. S. Eliot, was contributing its own fierce originality to the literary renaissance that had begun after World War I and would end with the outbreak of World War II. While W. H. Auden and Stephen Spender were leading a new generation of poets, novelists of Pritchett's generation—Elizabeth Bowen, George Orwell, Evelyn Waugh, Graham Greene, and Nancy Mitford—were carving a place for themselves alongside the already established moderns like Katherine Mansfield, Virginia Woolf, and D. H. Lawrence. Compared to the present day, this was a time of literary entrepreneurship, when small publishing houses were prepared to take chances with new and untried authors and when dozens of small literary magazines and even more established ones published avant-garde poetry and experimental stories. A young writer of Pritchett's

talent and dedication could often find in this climate an entrance to
the literary world by making connections with any of a number of the
coteries that enlivened London's literary scene. Edward O'Brien, the
influential editor of the annual Best British Short Stories series, advised Pritchett to cultivate friends among the Bloomsbury group, but
Pritchett had never heard of it and in any event had no interest in
coteries. He preferred then and throughout his career to go his own
way. Rather than settle in Bloomsbury as O'Brien advised, in 1930
Pritchett moved to Marlow, Buckinghamshire (VSP to ADP, 20
March 1930), where living was cheap and he could enjoy relative
peace and solitude.

Pritchett's move to the country is symbolic of his struggle
throughout the thirties to establish himself as a writer. Most of his
energies were devoted, of necessity, to writing endless reviews and
short articles for the *New Statesman,* the *Fortnightly Review,* the *Bystander,* and other magazines. As time permitted, he polished and revised his short stories and struggled to produce a novel that would
make his reputation. With few exceptions, however, the thirties was
a decade of frustration and disappointment. *Marching Spain* (1928)
had met with small success, and *Clare Drummer,* his first novel
(1929), sold fewer than one thousand copies. *The Spanish Virgin*
(1930) surprised everyone by selling nearly three thousand copies, a
remarkably high number for a short story collection by a little-known
author, but his next novel, *Shirley Sanz* (1932), was a commercial failure in both Britain and the United States, prompting publishers to
offer a smaller advance than usual for *Nothing Like Leather* (1934).
Pritchett's success in the short story was hardly much greater. Between 1930 and 1939 he published thirty-six stories in magazines
varying from the *Fortnightly Review,* the *New Statesman,* and *New
Writing* to *Nash's Magazine,* but his income from these probably did
not exceed £1,200, and the more unconventional stories often traveled to half a dozen or more editors before being published. By the
end of the decade Pritchett was writing some of the finest short fiction in England, including "You Make Your Own Life" (1937), "The
Sailor" and "The Clerk's Tale" (1939), and "The Saint" (1940), but
he reached this creative height just as the world was plunging into
war. [14]

The first half of the 1930s was as difficult personally as it was artis-
tically. His marriage to Evelyn, which had evidently not gone well
from the beginning, steadily deteriorated. In the spring of 1935 she

wrote to A. D. Peters, giving her address as Stanley Gardens, London; a month later, Pritchett wrote to his literary agent that he had moved to Rudall Crescent (Evelyn Pritchett to ADP, 26 March 1935; VSP to ADP, 26 April 1935). Quite possibly their separation occurred a few months after Pritchett had met Dorothy Roberts at a party on Guy Fawkes night (5 November) in 1934, where they fell instantly in love. In September 1936 divorce proceedings were completed, and shortly afterward Pritchett married Dorothy in the Hampstead Town Hall. He has always maintained that this change in his marital life was responsible for the improvement in his writing during the second half of the decade. "If I began to write better it was for two reasons: in my thirties I had found my contemporaries and had fallen happily and deeply in love. There is, I am sure, a direct connection between passionate love and the firing of the creative power of the mind" (*MO,* 221). This claim is substantiated not only by the short stories that followed 1936 but also by the last novel he would write for fifteen years, *Dead Man Leading* (1937), which in some ways is his most unified and successful, and certainly his most imaginative.

The improvement in Pritchett's personal life brought about by his marriage to Dorothy was offset at least partially by his father's final bankruptcy in 1936. This created an emotional strain and added a financial burden. With few assets apart from some money his wife had managed to hide over the years Walter Pritchett was forced to live on "loans" from his sons. Cyril, now well established in the silk trade, bore much of the burden, but years later Pritchett acknowledged that he had regularly supported his father since 1936.[15]

As already noted, Pritchett reached his potential as a short story writer late in the thirties, only to have his progress interrupted by the outbreak of World War II. The war was unkind to most writers, distracting them from their work, upsetting the machinery of book publishing and distribution, and disrupting the reading public. After some initial panic, however, publishers found that the British public had developed overnight a craving for books, and in spite of paper shortages, uncertain distribution, and the destruction of book stocks and libraries by the blitz, anything they printed sold out. This state of affairs was the making of some writers, but Pritchett was either unable or unwilling to take advantage of it. Had he published a novel or even a volume of stories, he might suddenly have found himself a best-seller, but the only book he issued during the war was a collection of critical essays, *In My Good Books* (1942). With two children to support (Josephine, born in 1938, Oliver in 1940) and a difficult country house to maintain (the Pritchetts had moved to Maiden Court in Berkshire in 1939), he devoted hours to tending a vegetable garden, chopping firewood, and hauling water. Nights were often spent on duty with the local farmers and laborers as part of the hastily organized and laughably ineffectual Home Guard. As the occupant of the "great house" of the neighborhood, he was also elected to the local Parish Council, but those who served with him report that little was accomplished because Pritchett distracted the group with droll and comic stories.[16] Like most writers, Pritchett was put to work by the military, though this aspect of his life is slightly mysterious. Apparently he was attached to the Ministry of Information, for many letters during the war years mention writing projects undertaken for it, among them *Build the Ships: The Official Story of the Shipyards in Wartime* (1946). That he wore a uniform is indicated by a letter to Gerald Brenan (11 August 1940); however, he did not receive writing assignments as military orders, for correspondence with A. D. Peters indicates that terms, subjects, and payments were negotiated through Pritchett's agent. Moreover, his MOI assignments left him relatively free to pursue other work, for in addition to writing official pamphlets and reports on shipping and transport, he appeared frequently on BBC radio to discuss books and writers.

These activities left little energy for writing fiction. He managed some slight pieces such as "The Invader," "Gold Fish," and "Cup Final" for the *New Statesman,* and one of his finest stories, "The Saint," appeared in 1940, but as the war dragged on, inspiration waned. By the middle of the decade he had hit a fallow period and actually gave up writing fiction for about two years, though there were enough stories from the late thirties and early forties to make up the collection *It May Never Happen* (1945). No novel appeared during the period at all. Most of his time was spent writing a weekly critical essay for the *New Statesman,* giving frequent talks on the BBC, and doing other jobs of literary journalism. His growing children were a pleasant distraction, and he visited nearly every week with Gerald Brenan, who was living close by in Aldbourne. They had met in the late thirties, and their shared enthusiasm for literature and passion for Spain formed the basis for a deep and lasting friendship.[17] Pritchett's published books during the 1940s reflect his preoccupation with criticism: *In My Good Books* (1942), *The Living Novel* (1946), and *Why Do*

I Write? (1948). As he himself pointed out, "If truth is the first casualty in war, the second is the literature of the period, especially reflective literature."[18] Despite the difficulties and frustrations of the war, Pritchett resented less the interruption of his career than feeling "imprisoned" in England. Travel in Europe was obviously out of the question, and visiting North America was almost impossible.

When Japan surrendered to the Allies in August 1945, Pritchett's connection with the Ministry of Information ended. During the war younger staff members of the *New Statesman* had been drafted away from their desks, so Pritchett was persuaded to become a full-time member of the staff in 1945 and moved up to literary editor in November 1947. He did not much enjoy editing: accustomed to the freedom of free-lance writing, he became restless when chained to a desk and restricted by regular hours. Financial pressures had been temporarily and partially alleviated the previous year by a legacy of £1,300 from Aunt Ida Bugg, which she probably left to him rather than to his mother to prevent Walter from getting his improvident hands on the money (VSP to GB, undated letter postmarked 1944). Nevertheless, Pritchett still could not concentrate on the novel he had been struggling with for some time, as writing and editing for the *New Statesman* left him very little time for anything else. By the end of 1947 he was privately complaining of the trivialities, headaches, and anxieties of the job (VSP to GB, 22 December 1947), though he conceded that to have a position that left some freedom to write was a blessing. He might have continued in this way indefinitely if Gerald Brenan had not stepped forward with an unusually generous offer: he would lend Pritchett five hundred pounds so that he could devote full time to his novel. Overwhelmed by Brenan's generosity, Pritchett was at first reluctant to accept. In a long letter that may have been as much catharsis for him as explanation to Brenan, he confessed that he had always written as a form of vengeance or hatred toward life and that his present novel *(Mr. Beluncle)* was in particular an attempt to adjust to hatred. Brenan's act of generosity and affection, therefore, would perhaps confuse him and disrupt the novel. Moreover, he added, he had always feared debt because of his Micawberish father, and to change at his time of life might be difficult. In the end, however, he could not resist the prospect of peace and leisure, and he accepted Brenan's offer (VSP to GB, 30 June 1948).

Predictably, the *New Statesman* could not easily replace Pritchett, so he was not relieved of editorial duties until the spring of 1949.

Even then, he remained a regular contributor, believing that he had to keep himself hard at work to accomplish anything at all. The old puritan attitude did not change with the prospect of leisure.

Brenan's loan did not work any magic, even after Pritchett had left the *New Statesman,* but it certainly breathed new life into a writer exhausted by overwork. The letters of 1949–50 take on a light, sometimes playful tone, for while Pritchett had always been known among his friends as a humorous, good-natured man, these qualities are not evident in his letters during the mid-forties. Renewed lightheartedness was perhaps the most immediate effect of Brenan's generosity. Its contribution to the novel is more difficult to assess, for Pritchett found writing *Mr. Benuncle* difficult technically, and he still claimed that every time he sat down to write, he had to learn all over again how to go about it (VSP to GB, 6 July 1949). After eighteen months of uninterrupted work he finished the book, even though he was disappointed with it (VSP to GB, October 1950). After this experience he never completed another novel. It is as if he had tested himself under ideal conditions—few distractions, monetary security, and domestic happiness—and found himself wanting. Fourteen years had elapsed since *Dead Man Leading,* during which time he had continually worked on short pieces—stories, essays, radio broadcasts, official reports. He was unused to sustained concentration and had never been comfortable with the problems of the novel's architecture. *Mr. Beluncle,* which he had hoped would establish him as a novelist, ironically proved to be his undoing.

Mr. Beluncle appeared in the fall of 1951 to mixed but generally favorable reviews, and three more books appeared before the decade closed, one in each of Pritchett's genres: *Books in General* (1953), *The Spanish Temper* (1954), and *Collected Stories* (1956). All were extremely well received, particularly *The Spanish Temper,* which drew lavishly positive notices from everyone. Nevertheless, the decade was to prove a repeat of the 1930s in two important respects. Having decided not to attempt another novel, Pritchett returned to the short story with renewed vigor. However, once again editors found his stories too difficult or plotless for all but the most sophisticated readers. Even the *New Yorker,* which had purchased first reading rights for Pritchett's short fiction during the fifties, sent back "Passing the Ball" for revisions and rejected "The Citizen" (1953), "The Snag" (1956), and "On the Scent" (1960).[19] For a writer of his experience and reputation, these rejections were discouraging.

The fifties also resembled the thirties in the difficulties of his personal life. Almost exactly twenty years after separating from Evelyn, he nearly divorced Dorothy. There had been serious problems for years preceding the crisis in the spring of 1955, when Pritchett briefly left Dorothy and took refuge in the Savile Club (VSP to GB, 12 March 1956). The problem arose from Dorothy's excessive drinking, which had been disrupting their lives for some time and had now culminated in a series of violent outbursts (VSP to GB, 18 December 1955). Complicating the situation further was the fact that Pritchett had fallen deeply in love with a married woman while serving as visiting professor at Princeton University in 1953. She arrived in London at the height of the crisis, intensifying his pain and sharpening their dilemma; however, after a great deal of agonized soul-searching, they decided that the trauma of two divorces was more than they could bear, and they agreed to end the affair (VSP to GB, 12 August 1955). Meanwhile, shocked by being left alone and urged by her doctor and friends to seek treatment, Dorothy finally agreed. This was eventually successful in all respects, and the two have remained together and untroubled ever since. Understandably, this is an episode that Pritchett has never mentioned publicly, but there is no doubt that it affected his writing. During the middle and late 1950s he published no new stories but took refuge in criticism and travel writing, two forms he could rely on for a steady income and could do while struggling with personal difficulties. Afterward, Pritchett looked back on these years as the most difficult of his life. "At 57, I looked despairingly bleak, ill and flaccid, to judge from a photograph, less brisk than I became in my 60's and 70's or today."[20] The stream of stories that appeared during the following two decades is testimony to the wholeness of the marriage once a reconciliation had been effected.

By the 1960s Pritchett had reached the age at which many authors retire, or if they do not, they probably should. Pritchett not only continued to write, but also produced some of his best work during this and the following decade. As in previous years, his output varied: three volumes of short stories, three travel books, three of criticism, and two of autobiography. In addition, he spent three academic years at American universities: Beckman Professor at the University of California, Berkeley, 1962; Writer-in-Residence at Smith College, 1966; Visiting Professor at Brandeis University, 1968. He also delivered the Clark Lectures at Cambridge University in 1969. Wherever he went,

he was a respected teacher and popular lecturer. One of those who
observed him in action at Brandeis describes him in these words:

At Brandeis Victor ran into the student revolt—his main impression was that
students in that epoch seemed very sad, without pleasure, delight: so he
taught a very large open public lecture series on 18th century "male knock-
about picaresque humor"—I remember Peacock especially. The students
were probably stunned at his delight—he read wonderfully and jumped
about, all quite unselfconsciously as he read and semi-acted the scenes from
18th and early 19th century novels. They applauded firmly: the thing was,
he offered them a totally unfamiliar, apparently "irrelevant" sort of literature, responded to with chuckling and bellowing relish—and it wasn't SERI-
OUS or Marxist or feminist but—and this was important—it *was* irreverent,
anti-establishment, ribald and keystone kopish matter delivered by a man
who just didn't fit their idea of a distinguished English lit. gent. He gave
them a present—delight, human warmth, not rage, at the spectacle we make
of ourselves. It relieved some of the burden of moral superiority, hostility
and wariness to the "over 30s" the now over 30s in his audience glumly lived
with as their generational baggage.[21]

These periods were mutually beneficial: American students and faculty were treated to Pritchett's critical insights and unabashed pleasure in literature, while he received a good salary and peace and quiet
in which to write. As he noted several times in letters to Gerald
Brenan, visiting professorships gave him more time than usual for
writing, in part because social distractions were fewer and also because he was released from his weekly obligation to the *New
Statesman.*

In contrast with the fifties, the sixties were relatively peaceful and
prosperous. Victor and Dorothy were able to travel to Europe, South
America, or the Near East nearly every year, either on holiday or under commission from a magazine. The children had grown up and
were comfortably settled. Josephine made a good marriage and bore
two children of her own. Oliver took his degree at Cambridge and
then launched a writing career as a journalist, beginning with a series
of jobs on small reviews and graduating eventually to the *Guardian.*
Dorothy was in good health, and Pritchett himself seems to have suffered no illness. The one serious blow came with the death of his father. Although Walter had been in many respects his son's enemy,
Pritchett felt a void in his life when his father—well into his eight-
ies—passed away, his dying words complaining that he had never
been given enough to eat (VSP to GB, undated).

The years since the publication of Pritchett's two volumes of auto-biography, *A Cab at the Door* (1968) and *Midnight Oil* (1971), have been quiet, prosperous, and rewarding. Pritchett has taken his place gracefully as the grand old man of British letters and has reaped rewards commensurate with his achievements. In 1969 he was made a Commander of the Order of the British Empire (C. B. E.), and in 1971 was elected president of the English P. E. N. Club, becoming its international president in 1974. The same year that group honored him with its award for nonfiction writing. He has received honorary D. Litt. degrees from the University of Leeds and Columbia. The American Academy of Arts and Letters made him an honorary member in 1971. These honors were capped in 1975 when he was knighted for his services to literature.

Such a profusion of honors might have convinced Pritchett to put his pen aside and bask in the glow of his accomplishments, but he is incapable of not writing. Most of his works in the past fifteen years have been nonfiction, but the books continue to come out in a steady stream: *Balzac* (1973), the *Gentle Barbarian: The Life and Work of Turgenev* (1977), the *Myth-Makers* (1979), the *Tale Bearers* (1980). In 1981 he edited the *Oxford Book of Short Stories*. The most recent collection of his own stories, *On the Edge of the Cliff*, appeared in 1979. In addition, two retrospective volumes, *Collected Stories* (1982) and *More Collected Stories* (1983), were greeted with high praise on both sides of the Atlantic and served to remind critics of his achievements in this genre. These works are in addition to the reviews he regularly contributes for the *New York Review of Books* and other periodicals. On his eightieth birthday journalists from numerous papers made the pilgrimage to his home on Regent's Park Terrace and were surprised to find him still at work, daily writing from morning to lunch time, from mid-afternoon until evening, seven days a week. Dorothy, surely the only person able to decipher his nearly illegible handwriting, has served now for years as his typist, advisor, and barrier against the literary hangers-on who would otherwise gather around.

Perhaps the only goal that has eluded him is popular success. None of his books has ever reached the best-seller lists, nor has he been able to exploit those other media of literary reputation, television and film. In 1984 one of his stories, "The Wedding," was filmed for television,[22] but one story is not enough exposure to create widespread interest. Numerous appearances on BBC radio and television have not made him a celebrity, either, for he can shop quite undisturbed in his neighborhood or frequent London pubs to eavesdrop on those who might become the subject of his next short story without fear of recognition. More surprising is his relative obscurity in academic circles. The two volumes of autobiography have been hailed as classics in their genre, and his stories have been widely reprinted and anthologized, yet he has not been included in the canon of standard authors whom students in high school or college read as part of their course work. The vagaries of literary politics are impossible to comprehend, but perhaps his failure to produce a major novel lies at the heart of his undeserved obscurity.

In spite of popular and critical neglect, Pritchett remains a gentleman of enormous humor and good will. Among the hundreds of reviews he has written over the years, not one has been foul-tempered or even testy, for he has deliberately chosen not to write about a book he dislikes. He is equally affable among friends. He enjoys a good joke, a witticism (though never a malicious jibe), a droll story, and good conversation. Short of stature, with a mischievous smile and a ready wit, he has sometimes been compared to a pixie or elf, his smiling face half hidden by a pipe and billows of smoke, topped by a wisp of thinning gray hair. He is above all a private man, who hates gossip and refuses to cooperate with would-be biographers or critics.

These are features not only of his private life, but of his art, also. His congeniality as a person and a critic is reflected in his stories and novels, which seek to understand rather than condemn. This, and the enormous psychic burden of his father, are the keys to understanding his development and appeal as a writer. He makes an important and accurate point about himself in *Midnight Oil:* "I have rarely been interested in what are called 'characters,' i.e. eccentrics; reviewers are mistaken in saying I am. They misread me. I am interested in the revelations of nature and (rather in Ibsen's fashion) of exposing the illusions or received ideas by which they live or protect their dignity" (*MO,* 227). Pritchett took from his painful childhood and the struggles of his youth a keen sense of the comic incongruities of life and made of them a humanism at once perceptive and sympathetic. In him the style and the man are truly one.

Chapter Two
Earliest Works

Marching Spain

One expects an author's first book to reveal considerable youthful clumsiness, whether from excessive devotion to a model or a rash attempt at originality. In his early Paris days Pritchett had emulated Stevenson and Belloc, seeking inspiration in endless walking. Nothing came of this activity at the time, but when the pressure to write a book became irresistible, he took Belloc's *Path to Rome* as a model.[1] The result, *Marching Spain* (1928), is especially odd, for Pritchett wrote it not because he had something to express, but because he needed to write a book—any book. The simplest solution at the time seemed to be a travel book, and since Spain held special fascination, he decided to return. His itinerary suggests that he had no reason to be there except to gather material, for the route he chose is arbitrary, almost pointless, something he is forced to admit to the first Spaniard who asks why he is walking from Badajoz to Leon:

> Now that was what I myself had not decided. The purposelessness of the journey was a constant worry to my conscience. . . . Remembering my line of march would be by the great Roman road, the Via Plata, and that by this line also Wellington advanced in the Peninsular War, I tossed up, as it were, the Roman road and the Duke in my mind, and decided for the Duke.[2]

As the book unfolds, however, neither the Duke nor the Via Plata figures significantly. A walking tour may be undertaken for its own sake, of course, but that is not Pritchett's purpose either. At the station in London he had seen a man selling shoe laces and matches, and had concluded, "We are all shops. I supposed, as we were sucked into the tube, I was going to sell Spain" (3). Had his aim been purely commercial, the book might be less eccentric, but his arbitrary route, confused motives, and the difficulties of writing his first book combined to make *Marching Spain* very unusual indeed.

Readers of travel books have a variety of interests. Some respond to the lure of exotic places, descriptions rich in local color, historic sites, strange terrain and costumes, and the unusual customs of other people. Others want social or political insights, or simply a guide to the picturesque. Casual tourists want information about historical sites, restaurants, hotels, and shops. Others respond to the personality of a particular travel writer. *Marching Spain* is directed at none of these audiences, which is another part of its strangeness. The route of the journey is indicative, for it suggests that Pritchett is not concerned about potential readers. His march takes him well to the west of prominent cities like Seville, Toledo, and Madrid, and there is nothing inviting about the scenery he encounters on his way: "No; I would keep to that harder central plateau, and I would know the monotony of that burned-up country, the dumbness of its cottages and taverns" (6). As the writer moves northward, he sees nothing to arrest the eye or soothe the senses. Pritchett gives us no stunning vistas or charming scenic sketches; he concentrates instead on poor soil, strange rock formations, austere landscapes, and the searing sun. Pritchett's Spain is harsh, barren, skeletal, poor. His is the journey not of the tourist or traveler, or even of the commentator or observer, but of the penitent. "It would be unpleasant for my body, but for the soul it would be ennobling" (6).

Had Pritchett given us a spiritual odyssey, he might have created a far more appealing and promising book, but there is no discernible change in the narrator. He remains for the most part acutely aware of physical suffering or at least of discomfort, but these are not transformed into moments of revelation. Rather, Pritchett conveys nothing so much as a tone of grim and even pointless determination, an obstinate effort to walk twenty miles a day at whatever cost with rarely a suggestion that he is enjoying or benefiting from his exertions. What we see, therefore, in addition to Pritchett's subjective view of Spain and the Spanish, is the country and its people filtered through the eyes of a pilgrim who projects his own aches and pains onto the scene before him. The book is not unrelievedly gloomy, but its dominant tone is sombre and bloody, a travelogue by a writer with aching feet and a blistered soul:

When I heard those words of the carabinero I knew at last I had touched Spain. We steamed out of La Coruna in a deepening blue heat, hot Spain lying to the east of us, its torrid, brown and sapphire slabs of land beyond a raw sea. The wide boat of black iron pushed forward and trod down the waves, and we were borne moodily in a dream of blue. In time the wind dropped and we began to feel the sun. He seemed to circle rampaging up in the sky. . . .

In the air's fire I could see the dark, sparkling figure of a horseman riding on a track through the lavender towards the inn. The inn was a pink wall outstaring the sun, a bitter wall, a strident wall, and in the centre was a black doorway bored into the glare. (25, 80)

In part Pritchett's tone is the result of immature prose, a striving after effects by laying on adjectives and searching always for the most violent word—"a strident wall . . . bored into the glare," a boat that "trod upon the waves," and a sun "rampaging up in the sky." However, there are also questions of point of view and sensibility, a consistent selection of harsh details and extremes of feeling, mostly negative.

These qualities are striking when compared with the style of a similar book, Laurie Lee's *As I Walked Out One Midsummer Morning*. Admittedly, Lee's book is nostalgic autobiography and thus may be colored by the rose-tinted glasses of time past, but in other respects the books are similar. Both concern journeys on foot by young men in their twenties, and at Zamora their paths cross. Lee writes:

I finally reached Zamora early one Saturday evening, after a blistering day through the wheat fields. The town stood neatly stacked on its rocky hill, a ripple of orange roofs and walls, somewhat decrepit now, but giving off something of the medieval sternness and isolated watchfulness of its past. Around its rocky site curled the track of the Douro, a leathery arm of wrinkled mud, laced down the middle with a vein of green water in which some half-naked boys were bathing.[3]

Pritchett writes:

We saw the white windows of Zamora shining, the vivid evening on its towers and westward houses, and the rest pooled in liquid shadow. Crossing the fishlike Duero, we flew climbing round the long wall and entered the town. . . .

    Beneath the walls the Duero is as yellow and green as a serpent, the second river of Spain. Like all the Spanish waters, it is low in the fierce summer when heat saps its strength to the bone, but in the winter it whelms into flood, and with the power of a dragon gnashes whitened jaws on the weirs and swells breast to breast with the bridges. (188–89)

Even though this is one of Pritchett's milder descriptions, the contrast is sharp. Lee's Zamora is "neatly stacked," and the words *ripple, curled, wrinkled,* and *laced* soften the effect of harsher adjectives like *decrepit* and *leathery.* Pritchett's serpent and dragon imagery, however, overwhelms the softer passage that precedes it, leaving the reader with a decidedly unpleasant impression of the city.

Not all of *Marching Spain* is harsh in tone and negative in outlook. There are humorous and charming portraits like that of "The King of Vigo," an outlandishly dressed customs official, and poignant moments, like the description of the lonely Basque woman who cannot communicate with her Castilian husband. Occasionally, Pritchett enjoys a joke at his own expense or relaxes to describe a lyrical scene. He is most effective when he can escape the burden of penance and simply present objectively the scene before him, as when he describes the colorful evening *paseo* (the nightly procession of people walking around the city square to see and be seen), the conversation of men in cafés, and the large, formal Spanish meals with their pungent food and, in one case, the disturbing presence of a beautiful woman, "dark as an Arab" (112), at whom all the men stare in appreciation. Similarly, when Pritchett allows the people to be themselves and simply talk, they come alive to reveal themselves and their country. Chapter 19, for example, provides a captivating and lively account of two ballad singers and their effect on the people of Zamora. The chapter following dramatically contrasts three scenes: the first Pritchett's encounter with a blind woman and her young grandchildren groping their way toward Zamora, the second a quiet but revealing discussion with a plowman, and the third a portrait of a village too poor and demoralized to welcome him. The most effective chapter in the book is the last. Here, calm, clear description replaces the purple prose of earlier pages, and the aggressive, angry tone that so often marked preceding chapters gives way to melancholy. As he enters Leon after eighteen days of walking, he laments that 340 miles traveled are "not very good going" (222).

Pritchett's sense of relief at the end suggests that, contrary to his professed intent, the journey was physical, not spiritual. It is hard to escape the feeling that much of his bad temper and sour disposition results from too much sun, bad food, and fatigue. Peace comes with the end of the body's trials. Pritchett nowhere acknowledges this, but the book appears to argue that suffering is *not* good for the soul. Spain's peasants are not ennobled by their poverty, nor are they corrupted by it. For them it is a fact of life, to be borne stoically or not, depending on their character. For his part, Pritchett is tired of a monotonous diet of eggs fried in olive oil, of straw mattresses infested by fleas, of sour wine and sore feet. If there is any "spiritual" discovery here, it is that the author is a solid middle-class Englishman, prepared to endure hardship if necessary but not to live the simple life for its own sake or its presumed moral benefits. Herein we find a clue to Pritchett's character and art, his lifelong concern with the battle between the spiritual and material. Normally we expect writers to come down on the side of the spiritual, but Pritchett had had his fill of spirituality as a young man influenced by his father's Christian Science. He prefers the concrete and material, although he also rejects the blatant greed that was the other side of his father's personality. Spain in general, and the experiences of *Marching Spain* in particular, helped Pritchett to perceive this truth about himself and those around him—that the middle-class struggle between the material and the spiritual was a drama worthy of his attention.

Overall, then, *Marching Spain* is not a success, its momentary insights and brief passages of good writing being insufficient to atone for its generally strained writing and lack of purpose. Pritchett has since disowned it. Today, its main interest lies in the meager light it sheds on Pritchett himself and in the contrast it provides with his later writing.

Clare Drummer

Clare Drummer (1929), Pritchett's first novel, derives from his experiences as a correspondent in Ireland during the early Republican days of 1923 and 1926. Although there are some superficial similarities between its protagonist, David Tremble, and the youthful Pritchett, the novel does not appear to be autobiographical. Rather, it attempts to capture the aura of uncertainty and nervousness of a people and nation shattered by civil war.

There is no strong story line in *Clare Drummer,* for the book is more a succession of incidents and emotional states than a well-plotted novel. Most episodes focus on Tremble, an ex-member of the notorious British Black and Tans, who has remained in Ireland after the war and has held a series of part-time, ill-paying jobs. Tremble is not very convincing as an ex-soldier, for he is all nerves and indecision, not from shell shock but by disposition. When the book opens, he is once again out of work, but by chance he meets a former acquaintance, Mrs. Drummer, who delights in filling her damp and crum-

bling home with protégés of various sorts, none of whom ever turns
out to be of any use. She acquires for him the job of revising and
updating an Irish travel guide, but during the several months of the
novel's action we rarely see him at work on the book. Instead, he
spends most of his time with Mrs. Drummer's twenty-seven-year-old
daughter Clare and her friend Julia Macey. Both young women are in
love with Oriel Enctrury, described as "slender, excitable yet remote,
and effeminate young man you might see in a fashion plate."[4] Oriel's
effeminacy extends beyond mannerisms; marriage repels him, and
"the whole action of human generation was beneath him" (143). Clare
and Julia, therefore, are doomed to frustration, as is Tremble, who
first takes a fancy to Julia and then falls indecisively in love with
Clare. Whether he is truly in love with her is impossible to deter-
mine, for Tremble is a weak, ineffectual, and sometimes morbid character who seldom knows his own mind. His proposal to Clare (which
she rejects) carries little conviction, though he is angry and hurt at
being turned down. One of the mysteries of *Clare Drummer* is why the
two women spend so much of their time with Tremble, who has few
attractions apart from a certain pathetic quality and a superficially
agreeable manner.

When not detailing some aspect of this futile love quadrangle, the
novel focuses on the painful lives of three members of the Drummer
household. Clare is moody, impetuous, energetic, and anxious to
spend as much time as possible away from her parents. Mrs. Drummer, when not encouraging protégés, is nominally in charge of her
deteriorating house Roscullagh, but she is too flighty to manage it
efficiently. Colonel Drummer, retired from the army, tries to salvage
some measure of order and masculine dignity from the female chaos.
His obsessions are the mail boat that plies the channel between England and Ireland, which he can see from his window, and the order
and repose of his own room, where he has installed a grand piano.
Late in the novel he breaks his leg and, although the leg mends, he
dies because he has lost the will to live. The only servant characterized in detail is the colonel's only friend, Swift, who spends his free
time writing letters to imaginary friends in America.

The interactions and interior struggles of these characters do not
yield a theme in the conventional sense so much as a general atmosphere of frustration that at times approaches insanity. Hovering over
the novel is a malevolent cloud that has no apparent source and that

no sun can dissipate. The characters are trapped, although whether by character or circumstances is unclear, for little of Ireland and less of society impinge upon them. Pritchett's decision to concentrate on a small cast and his reluctance to set them solidly in a social context give the novel a claustrophobic air.

It would be exaggerating to say that *Clare Drummer* is dominated by doom. In fact, some Faulknerian sense of inevitable decay or overpowering fate would be an asset. Instead, there is simply a feeling of morbidity and squalor. The opening pages establish this in a series of peculiar images. Mrs. Drummer has "bluish-silvery yellow skin" and white hair "thrown back from the forehead in one white blast . . . Many people had thought momentarily they had seen her hollow skull . . ." (14–15). The harbor on Drummer's property is "built in a creek, the green water daggered in a heap of gigantic bleached skulls" (13). Clare herself has a voice "as shrill as glass," and when she climbs a rock to dive into the water, she is "like some sharp solid insect" (16). Later, she emerges from her swim "dragging the heavy sheet of sea she had ripped with her. A thin branch of watery blood was spread on her skin . . ." (20). Part of the problem here is overwriting, a fault of the novel throughout, but beyond this one has to ask what function such imagery serves. It seems gratuitous and inappropriate to the characters or the situation in Ireland, which is occasionally alluded to as unpleasant. None of the characters can be called malicious, but all are flawed and incomplete. The dominant impression such imagery conveys is that of a young writer striving for originality and naturalism but lacking a coherent sense of purpose for this supposed toughness.

Nevertheless, the book is not entirely without merit. Although the characters are unattractive, all are portrayed vividly enough to make them seem genuine at least part of the time. Tremble is complex, sometimes intriguing, but also too obviously inept and ineffectual, making one wonder how he survived the war and why Mrs. Drummer would show an interest in him. Yet, when we see beneath his social bewilderment and emotional confusion we find a basic if vacillating decency. Tremble is modern neurotic man, not strong or interesting enough to qualify as an antihero, but recognizable as a common casualty of the twentieth century. Morally and psychologically he is confused by the world, uncertain of his place in it, longing for stability and affection, but constitutionally unable to achieve any of these. He is particularly sympathetic late in the book when he seems to be in love with Clare, who uses him as a surrogate for Oriel. "She had proved to herself that she was capable of arousing love, confident for a few hours at least that, encouraged, enriched, empowered by it, she might win Enctrury yet" (305). Finally, however, Tremble rejects her, for by the time she realizes that her affection for Enctrury is pointless, Tremble has lost his job and is leaving Dublin for Belfast. Moreover, having been repeatedly rejected, he finds the chance at revenge irresistible and so leaves Dublin in precisely the position we first met him, except that now he is frightened by love as well as war and poverty.

Clare is much more appealing than Tremble, particularly early in the book. Burdened by a mother whose chief aim in life is to use and control her, and saddled with a hopeless love for Oriel, she arouses sympathy. Her energy and pluck are also appealing, as are her spontaneous gaiety and natural enthusiasm. "Clare Drummer came in with a letter. She took long comical steps across the room, rolling her eyes and making grotesque gestures. Tremble laughed. She danced towards him, separating her arms, swaying. Kicking her legs out, turning her toes in and advancing towards him, tapped him on the head with the letter. Mrs. Drummer and Tremble shook with laughter at this dumb show" (61). A moment later, however, she is gloomy with the realization that she is "always *nearly* doing things" and never mastering or completing anything. Perhaps this is why her morning swims take on a hard and compulsive quality, lacking joy or pleasure. Like nearly all Pritchett's young characters during this period, Clare is intensely preoccupied with herself and subject to violent swings of mood, but her hopeless love for Oriel does not make her likable. Not only does it dominate her life and lead to blatant exploitation of Tremble's affection (such as it is), but also it finally drives her to run aimlessly from home. Her flight might appear as admirable defiance or as an attempt at independence had its motive been rational choice rather than futile desperation.

Of the remaining characters, the men are more successful. Julia is seen only briefly, enough to establish her as a schemer and snob. Mrs. Drummer is selfishly manipulative but otherwise incompetent. Her husband is interesting in his neuroses: unable to assert any authority in his home, he retreats into a private world of bitter complaints, compulsive neatness, and emotional isolation. In the end, he is defeated by the feminine world of "Gossip, disorder, screaming, extravagance, lying, madness, religion" (73). In contrast to him is Julia Macey's overbearing and puritanical father, obsessed by social position and material advantage—an early portrayal of Pritchett's father.

Structurally, the book is loose and uneven. Some scenes are extremely well handled, and even this early Pritchett shows a keen ear for dialogue and a good sense of pacing and rhythm in dramatic moments. One very good scene occurs when Tremble and Clare are walking in the country and witness a field being burned so that hunters can slaughter the rabbits and birds. Clare responds with pity and outrage, while Tremble ineffectually sympathizes instead of confronting those perpetrating the cruelty. The scene has a nightmarish physical quality and suggestive moral dimension that could make it a central event in the novel, but Pritchett, having described it and his characters' immediate reactions, does no more with it. Similarly, two dramatic scenes between Clare and Tremble present first a malicious physical battle and then a verbal sparring match of raw, tangled emotions. Few young novelists have so convincingly portrayed the violence and complex emotions aroused by thwarted love. However, in spite of their momentary power, these scenes reveal no new dimensions of the characters, nor do they connect organically to the novel as a whole. Between such dramatic moments are numerous dry patches that contribute little beyond bulk. In particular, chapter 8 seems wholly superfluous, gratuitously bitter, and purposeless.

Clare Drummer is an uneven first novel of more ambition than accomplishment. Pritchett attempts to capture the listlessness and ennui of Ireland and its people in the years following a debilitating civil war, but though there are notable passages and excellent scenes, the book does not cohere. Its characters, despite vivid moments, are figures in a shadow drama, cut off from their surroundings and their society. If we knew a great deal more about Pritchett's experiences in Ireland, particularly his courtship of Evelyn Vigors, the novel might have more biographical interest. A hint to this effect comes in a letter to A. D. Peters, in which Pritchett jokes that by bringing Evelyn to London with him, he might help to keep her from drowning herself for one day at least.[5] Since Clare Drummer is an avid swimmer who nearly drowns at one point in the novel, this hint, plus the fact that both women are Irish, suggests that Evelyn may have been the model for Clare. Whatever the precise biographical connection between Prit-

chett and his novel, it served as the starting point for his career as a
novelist and, in some quarters, advanced his reputation as a young
man to watch.

The Spanish Virgin

Pritchett's first volume of short fiction, *The Spanish Virgin and Other
Stories* (1930), consists of ten short selections and the novella-length
title piece, written specifically for the collection. The shorter pieces
were published previously in the *Irish Statesman,* the *Manchester
Guardian, Cornhill, Everyman,* the *New Statesman,* and other periodicals. Taken as a whole, the book is not remarkable, but it shows Pritchett experimenting with various styles and approaches in an effort to
find a voice. As first collections go, it is comparable to those of Pritchett's young contemporaries, like H. E. Bates, William Plomer, and
Elizabeth Bowen, but he has since disowned the book by refusing to
include any of its stories in later collections. This is unfortunate, not
only because early stories have a freshness and interest of their own,
but also because at least two are genuinely good.

The title story, however, is not one of Pritchett's best. It bears the
marks of a tale written to fill space—loose in structure, slack in style,
and vague in purpose. The basic material comes from his meeting a
Mrs. Lang and her daughter Judy in Paris, which he described in
Midnight Oil. Pritchett transfers the setting from Paris to Seville, and
his part is that of a young engineer rather than an aspiring author.
Otherwise, the characters and situation are fairly true to Pritchett's
experience.

The material for "The Spanish Virgin" is potentially rich: the Edwardian mother living in a dream world while using her beautiful and
unsuspecting daughter as bait to extort "loans" from her admirers has
all the elements of a penetrating study of individual psychology and
social mores. However, Pritchett spins his tale out at too great a
length; what might have been an excellent story of thirty pages loses
impact when dragged out to over one hundred and sixty. It succeeds
best while set in Seville. The mother's aristocratic pretensions, the
daughter's innocence, the cultural clash between the English women
and the Spanish men who are aroused by the freedom of British mores, and the perplexity of Alec Ferguson (Pritchett's alter ego) make
lively reading. When Pritchett moves Mrs. Lance and Crystal to London, however, and takes us on the rounds of Crystal's fruitless search

for acting jobs, the story becomes dull and trivial. Still later, when Crystal is on tour with a third-rate acting company, the love scenes between her and the actor Fontenoy Dufaux read like passages of Edwardian melodrama. Pritchett even resorts to the device of the fainting spell and illness after an emotional shock. There is a momentary reawakening of interest at the end when Crystal is worn down by the attentions of Mr. Geelong and reluctantly marries him after her mother has become the mistress of the wealthy Mr. Trellis. The irony falls flat.

Two stories, however, are quite accomplished. "Greek Theatre Tragedy" is a study of artistic integrity, or rather its loss, revolving around a painter, William Bantock, who arrived in Sicily as a young man and became enthralled with the "naif intuition of infinity" that he saw in the Greek theater with Mount Etna rising in the background. He spent a lifetime attempting to capture that feeling on canvas, and in some of his paintings one could see that "there was a *flash* of greatness . . . ; he must have once had the fire."[6] However, artistic intuition and creative fire are poorly understood, particularly by those of the bourgeoisie like John Puigi, the English-Italian hotel keeper who shrewdly led Bantock by a series of timely hints to paint suitcase-sized pictures of the theater and Etna that would sell to tourists. Under his influence, Bantock dwindles into cliché, churning out thousands of paintings on the same subject, believing that he is pursuing the essence of the Greeks when in fact he is promoting Puigi's hotel. Pritchett masters this material, telling his story through a narrator who has pieced it together from observation and hearsay and who thus must re-create scenes from hints and incomplete evidence. The shifts in time and the tentative speculations about events and motives give the story a Jamesian complexity and aura of uncertainty that increase its power and appeal. Above all, Pritchett handles his theme with individuality and insight. Bantock does not consciously sell out, nor does Puigi deliberately ruin the artist. Puigi's commercial mind can see nothing but boasting in Bantock's attempts to describe his experience of the theater with words like *immensity, Powers,* and *Presences.* His middle-class practicality sees only the commercial potential in pictures that sell. What else are they for? With pride, Puigi says, "He owed his success to me. I made him." That is true, but only in an ironic sense that Puigi can neither understand nor appreciate. Bantock allows himself to be seduced by Puigi's suggestions, believing he is following his vision with single-minded integrity. In all, "Greek Theatre Tragedy" is a fine parable about the bourgeois and artistic temperaments and about the influence of money on art.

If "Greek Theatre Tragedy" is a parable, "The White Rabbit" suggests a beast fable. Set in a pretentious middle-class London neighborhood, it explores the hollow inner lives of its subjects, the Goughs. Every household has its running battle. For the Goughs, conflict centers on the children and their starchy governess, Miss Spencer, three times seduced and jilted by married men who at the last moment returned to their wives. Like Mr. Gough, Miss Spencer favors "intelligence" and "practicality," by which they mean a life of emotionless inflexibility in which people are objects. Mr. Gough thinks of his children this way: "For one of these days, when there was more leisure, he was going to devote a lot of time solely to intelligence; also he was reserving some vague cycle of gilded years for the love of his children and for the enjoyment of their gratitude. . . . Until then, until this late baptism of accumulating paternal affection, they were in limbo, as good as damned, and he meant 'damned' when he said it" (199). Opposing them is Mrs. Gough, who takes a queenly attitude toward the governess, biding her time until Miss Spencer makes some fatal mistake and the children will be her own once again. Pritchett works out their conflicts and suggests the outcome through the white rabbit and by using animal imagery to suggest human parallels.

The plot of the story is simple: rising early one morning, Mr. Gough discovers that his son Geoffrey has once again let his pet rabbit sleep in his bed. Gough seizes the animal by its ears and throws it outside. Later, while the Goughs are eating breakfast, the children lock themselves in the bathroom—their refuge of peace and security—and Miss Spencer is in her room, gazing idly out the window, pointedly ignoring the children's rebellion. As she watches, the family cat, whom the children have secretly named Spencer, stalks and kills the white rabbit.

The symbolism is clear enough. The rabbit in its innocence represents the permissive world of Mrs. Gough and the children themselves. The cat represents reality and Miss Spencer's theory of child rearing, for she feels "*morally bound* to estrange the children from their mother" (202). A victim herself of predatory males, she has become callous, identifying with the cat while officially hiding behind impartiality, both in her treatment of the children and as she watches the cat stalk the unsuspecting rabbit. Mr. Gough is characterized as "a gorilla covered in little black hairs" (205). When the cat attacks the rabbit, Miss Spencer belatedly cries out to the children, who in turn scream to their mother:

"Mummy! Mummy! Spencer's killed the rabbit. Spencer's killed the rabbit."
Miss Spencer drew her head in, listening. What—what was the child crying? (216)

Spencer has killed the rabbit in two senses, and this ambiguity gives this story its power, quite apart from the vividness of its characters and the tension that builds throughout. Here again is the villainous father figure, Walter Pritchett in slightly different dress, bullying and emotionally starving his children. The predatory family is a permanent part of Pritchett's vision, seen here in an early but very effective form.

The other stories in the collection are less successful but indicative of future directions and concerns. "Fishy," for example, is a comic sketch—two Irishmen bluffing one another, covering ignorance and poverty with blarney. "The Petrol Dump" is also set in Ireland and is full of local color, though its point is difficult to grasp. "In the Haunted Room" is an amusing and clever ghost story that leaves the reader smiling over the author's sleight of hand rather than frightened or amazed. "Rain in the Sierra," Pritchett's first published story, suffers from transparently overwrought folksiness and heavy-handed irony, while "A Sack of Lights" is imitation Maupassant with too little toughness and too much sentimentality. "The Corsican Inn" contains excellent descriptive writing; however, atmosphere is nearly all there is. Of autobiographical interest is "The Cuckoo Clock," a fusion of several boyhood memories into one terrifying experience. Here, Victor's Aunt Lax becomes Aunt Helen, and the fictional Uncle Ben is an amalgam of a number of Pritchett's northern puritanical relatives, especially his grandfather. In the story the boy is fascinated by his aunt and uncle's cuckoo clock, which mocks the uncle's stern catechizing and his efforts to keep ahead of time. It attracts the boy because it is the only colorful and frivolous thing in that well-scrubbed house. Climaxing the story is an event traumatic for young Victor: in an attempt to teach him the meaning of "Thou shalt not kill," his uncle loaded the shotgun and forced the terrified boy to point it at his aunt. The gun accidentally fires, blowing the cuckoo clock to smithereens. That night, the boy dreams of a falling cherry blossom. "But as he stooped to pick it up it blew away from him like the surf of the sea till only one petal was left, and it became a little shrivelled-up dead cuckoo with all its feathers off" (279).

Pritchett repeats the shotgun episode almost verbatim in *A Cab at the Door* (49–55), indicating the impact it had on his imagination. The cuckoo symbolizes the antipuritanism that drove Pritchett from his family. Ironically, he could never fully escape parts of that ethic, particularly the drive toward hard work, yet the attractive frivolity of the cuckoo and Pritchett's fear that something would kill it drew him to the bohemian life of the writer, where he spent much of his creative energy analyzing the puritanism he had tried to escape.

Chapter Three
The Struggling Novelist
Shirley Sanz

Throughout the thirties Pritchett devoted himself to building on the small reputation he had earned from *Marching Spain, Clare Drummer,* and *The Spanish Virgin*—pinning his hopes on fiction but relying on journalism for his daily bread. It is difficult to link Pritchett with any literary movement or ideology, not only because his autobiography is mute on such points but also because he appears to have remained deliberately aloof from literary circles. *Marching Spain,* written vaguely under the influence of Belloc and Stevenson, is a loner's book, while *Clare Drummer* fits loosely into the tradition of the realistic novel. If any precursors may be identified, they would be the novels of Conrad, particularly in the use of dense atmospherics and moral ambiguities. Pritchett's second novel, *Shirley Sanz,* appeared in 1932 (American title *Elopement into Exile*). This time the primary influence is Flaubert's *Madame Bovary,* both in the portrait of Shirley Sanz as a romantic and dreamer and in the novel's attempt at objectivity. Arnold Bennett's *Old Wives' Tale,* with its parallel stories of two women, might have served as a model for the structure of *Shirley Sanz.* The fact that Pritchett apparently derived his inspiration from Flaubert rather than from contemporary experiments in fiction indicates the distance that separated him from the modernist movement. Just the year previous Virginia Woolf had published *The Waves,* and in the same year *Shirley Sanz* appeared Aldous Huxley produced *Brave New World.* Beside these, *Shirley Sanz* appears tame and conventional.

Like *Clare Drummer, Shirley Sanz* is slightly autobiographical, deriving from Pritchett's experiences in Spain. One episode, the stoning of a Protestant chapel by Catholic fanatics, appeared in *Marching Spain,* but otherwise the novel's plot and characters seem creations of imagination rather than experience. It could be described as a novel about the clash of English and Spanish cultures, but Pritchett's aim is less to portray national characteristics than to dramatize these differences as they occur in individuals, particularly the central male characters, James Gordon and Lewis Sanz, partners in an import-export business. James is English in temperament: cool, businesslike, aloof, progressive. He exemplifies British colonial attitudes. By contrast, Lewis's roots and loyalties are Spanish. He dislikes business, is not interested in money, takes a casual attitude toward progress and expansion, and retains a personal interest in his employees. In many ways he would prefer to remain on his family estate, growing grapes and pressing wine without the distractions of commerce. Pritchett describes him as "patient, blunt, caustic, quick-witted" and "sedulously polite, simple, ironical, disparaging."[1]

This pair of opposites is paralleled by another, Shirley Goatham and Cynthia Harte. Shirley, like Madame Bovary, longs for romance, passion, and adventure. The great act of her life is to flee the security of home in Fennel Bridge, follow Lewis Sanz to London, and there induce him to marry her and take her to Spain. Having accomplished this, she is happy for a time adjusting to a new life in a strange country, and before these novelties wear off, she has the distraction and pleasure of her first child. After two years elapse, however, she again becomes restless. Life in the country is dull; the heat is oppressive; there is little society apart from Lewis's family; Spanish decorum forbids her the pleasures of Nerida's cafés. Lewis is too easygoing and ironical to take his childlike wife seriously. Perhaps because Shirley pursued and wooed him, he takes her love for granted, whereas she needs courtship and romance. Not surprisingly, Shirley sees in James many of the qualities lacking in her husband and, without being fully conscious of her intent, becomes attracted to him. Eventually, she and James make love. Lewis discovers her infidelity and for once becomes passionately angry. Shirley, having had her grand adventure in eloping with Lewis and her great sin in adultery with James, finds solace in romantic renunciation.

Cynthia, by contrast, is a hard-bitten woman of experience. We first meet her as she is being deserted by her lover, John Berger. Berger is Cynthia's grand passion, and she never recovers from his rejection. Still, she is practical enough to accept the attentions of Geoffrey, a fellow boarder in Mrs. Minty's eccentric house, and to entice him into accompanying her to Nerida, where she has vague hopes of reuniting with John. Like Shirley, she takes a daring chance, refusing to return to England but remaining in Spain where she suffers through a succession of jobs and men until she meets Shirley on a train and is hired as nurse and maid. In the course of the two years she is with Shirley, Cynthia becomes attracted to James, but by this time she is ambivalent about men and somewhat jaded. She and Shirley have reached virtually the same place by different routes.

The interactions of these four characters form the basis for most of the plot, which seems to be a cross between *Madame Bovary* and the Cain and Abel story set against a background of pre–Civil War Spain. Pritchett succeeds well with his characters. All four are reasonably complex and rounded, capable of surprise and change, individual in speech and habits, and mixtures of good traits and bad. They are worthy components of a family saga, but individually are not psychologically rich and complex enough to engage our imaginations fully.

The book might have been saved by a sound plot or an interesting theme, but the plot relies too heavily on coincidence and isolated incidents, while no theme emerges as a unifying idea. The clash between James and Lewis over the direction of the business provides every opportunity for Pritchett to explore the clash of cultures, questions of business ethics, or the tension between old values and new. Each idea is raised briefly, but Pritchett does not develop these conflicts or explore their ramifications. Overall, *Shirley Sanz* is less good than the sum of its parts. Its style is lively and controlled, its characters substantial, and many of its individual scenes are intensely realized. There is even new clarity and power in the descriptive passages, which range in effect from the brutal to the lyrical. Nevertheless, it remains an apprentice novel, valuable primarily to its author as a testing ground for fictional techniques that would later produce more substantial works.

Nothing Like Leather

Pritchett's third novel, *Nothing Like Leather* (1935), is the first to use what we now recognize as his typical material. The book is heavily autobiographical, taking characters and incidents from his years in the leather trade and endowing its protagonist, Mathew Burkle, with a blend of Pritchett's own personality and that of his father. Its literary ancestors are the middle-class epics of Bennett, but even more so H. G. Well's *The History of Mr. Polly* (1910), whose central character, like Pritchett's, is a dreamy, aspiring merchant. In this satire of bourgeois values and mores Pritchett echoes the sentiments of his antifascist contemporaries like W. H. Auden, Stephen Spender, and George Orwell, but his point of view is essentially unpolitical.

Rather, he is interested in his protagonist's shallow morality and lack of self-awareness. Thus, even though Pritchett may have shared some of the ideas of radical writers of the 1930s, his approach, as always, was his own. Perhaps the novel closest in spirit to *Nothing Like Leather* is Sylvia Townsend Warner's *The Flint Anchor* (1954).

Whatever its literary origins and affinities, *Nothing Like Leather* marks an advance in coherence and imaginative unity over the previous novels, in part because the book focuses on the career of Mathew Burkle, and in part because Burkle is a character Pritchett knows intimately. His speech, mannerisms, and motivations are rendered in detail. Whereas Clare Drummer and Shirley Sanz were sometimes vague and disembodied, Burkle is solid and particular. Mathew Burkle begins as a clerk in Petworth's country tannery, falls in love with the owner's daughter (although he does not marry her), and, after a lifetime's hard work, acquires a considerable fortune and a leather factory of his own in London. His ultimate goal, however, is to supplant the Petworths: "That dream of himself in possession of that place, a successor of the Petworths, the country tanner and country gentleman, was modest enough but it had an irresistible romantic glamour for him."[2] As he is about to realize this ambition, he falls into a tanning pit and drowns. More important than the similarities between young Mathew Burkle and Victor Pritchett are those between the mature Burkle and Walter Pritchett. Both are selfish and self-centered, fond of lavish spending, socially conscious, neglectful of their families yet unable to allow the children to exist independently. Like Walter Pritchett, Mathew Burkle is really married to his business, and his partner, Henrietta Petworth, plays a role very similar to that of Miss H, Walter's partner in the upholstery business.

The theme of *Nothing Like Leather* is announced in the first chapter: "Take a man, skin him, put the skin into the soak of work and watch the rest of him flutter away in the black flag of smoke" (3). Like many novels about business, this one explores the effects of commercialism and greed. It is a novel of middle-class ambition, mores, and values, although Burkle's initial ambition to become a successful country tanner represents a dream with at least a modicum of social conscience, for the man Burkle wants to supplant is no robber baron but an astute businessman who, at least by his own lights, is a useful citizen and civic benefactor, having founded institutions for working men and served three times as mayor. Petworth may be part humbug, but he is a long way from the new breed of businessman represented by the rapacious Montrey, an American speculator who acquires everything he can for the sake of making vast sums of money. Burkle falls between these extremes. He is also a puritan, but a puritan run amok, unable to conceive of spiritual or moral values except as aspects of the material: "Burkle did not regard himself as being like other men . . . , but he could not *afford* to live as most of his fellows lived, he could not *afford* to think of those things which lay on either side of the straight road he had been obliged to make for his life" (123).

Burkle's emotional limitations are related to sexual repressions and attitudes that he never masters nor understands. At the beginning of the novel the rakish Geoffrey Chappleman invites Burkle to join him in a drink at the Bell Hotel where the beautiful barmaid Daisy confuses and embarrasses Mathew just by talking to him. Months later, after his shy and hesitant attentions have resulted in a night in Daisy's bed, he can neither accept nor understand what has happened: "It was beautiful; it was horrible. Beauty and horror mingled inseparably, suavely engrained, a lowering of himself into slime!" (31). After this, he does not return to the Bell but begins to court Dorothy, the only daughter of a socialist photographer and dreamer. He maintains a purely platonic relationship with her, taking long walks, talking endlessly about ideal and spiritual love, and denying that sexual passion has any place in their affection. Throughout their courtship, however, Burkle is also attracted to Henrietta Petworth and finds himself thinking without shame that while Dorothy is heir to a small photography shop, Henrietta will inherit a tannery. However, Burkle cannot recognize his physical passions nor his material aspirations. Denying his own motives, he makes a unsuccessful marriage with Dorothy that gives neither the physical satisfaction Daisy might have provided nor the material benefits Henrietta could offer. Burkle's puritanism is not simply an aversion to the appetites of the flesh; it is mixed with romanticism and a general obtuseness about himself and others.

In contrast to the puritanical Burkle is Petworth's nephew, the playboy Geoffrey Chappleman. After Petworth dies, Chappleman manages the leather factory successfully for four years, during which time Mrs. Petworth and Henrietta daily hope that he will propose to her, but he remains strangely indifferent. He undergoes a radical change, moreover, when he discovers that Daisy has borne an idiot child. He had eased his conscience by giving her money and thinking that she was happily married to a publican, but seeing the child sickens him. Chappleman falls seriously ill, weakened in spirit, "not by guilt but by horror" (124).

Burkle's response to Chappleman's illness highlights their differences, for Burkle could alleviate his friend's suffering by confessing that he had slept with Daisy, but he cannot acknowledge his possible guilt. Instead, he improvises a test for God when, while skating, he hears the sickening sound of ice cracking beneath his feet: "If the ice does not break and I do not drown then I am not the father of Daisy's child; it will be a sign from God" (127). The ice holds and Burkle considers himself exonerated. On his next visit to Chappleman, Burkle decides that the sick man has been "chosen to bear this burden of guilt" (137) and even goes so far as to invest him with the qualities of "Jesus gathering into himself the vices of Burkle and annulling them" (138). This vision of Chappleman as sacrificial lamb is curiously joined to a peculiar brand of social Darwinism, for Burkle decides that Chappleman's duty is to carry the spiritual burden and his own is to bear the material. "And this, in the course of months, came to mean that Chappleman's burden was not important, it could not be reckoned in terms of substance or money and that Burkle's was the only burden. Relieved of his sins he could expand and act. . . . This was the way of life which preferred the strong to the weak" (138–39). Still, a residue of guilt remains until Chappleman asks Burkle how a supposedly good God could allow an idiot child to be born. "It is not God's will,' said Burkle mechanically and then light warmed and illuminated his heart. He had spoken the words which made him free, free of evil and free of the obligation to confess" (162). This contest of wills between a man who is physically ill and one who is spiritually impoverished is central to Pritchett's conception, but it ends with a non sequitur, for there is no discernible reason why Burkle should suddenly feel absolved. The key to Burkle remains a mystery, not only to himself but also to readers. Vital clues have been withheld as Pritchett has taken us only so far and then abruptly drawn back.

There are similar problems with the other characters. Dorothy's insistence on spiritual love disappears after marriage and is replaced by a querulous jealousy of Burkle's work and his relationship with Henrietta. We are told, "Her passion had no relation to fact, but to her inner need of an enemy and a drama by means of which her most profound instinct could warn him from a perverse way of life" (220), but this bears no resemblance to the Dorothy we met in the early chapters. Henrietta is equally mysterious. For years she clings to a hopeless love for Chappleman, which is plausible enough, but why are there no suitors for this beautiful and wealthy young woman? Long after Chappleman moves to France, she falls in love with a younger man, but he is killed. Later, she becomes the mistress of an engineer named Robinson, but for years before these involvements she had apparently lived like a nun, unaccountably separated from males. Her isolation seems more a convenient plot device than an integral part of her character. Chappleman too displays inexplicable contradictions. His sudden fall from playboy to invalid supposedly resulted from his horrified reaction to the idiot child, but late in the book Pritchett tells us that the child was not the real cause of his illness: "His life in England had become bankrupt and he had been able to run away. He had quickly recovered from his breakdown about the news of the idiot child, for that was merely a symbol of his trouble and not the cause of it; soon a new life had begun; a new life meant new places and new places meant for him—women" (373). Pritchett adds that Chappleman tired of women, then of his vineyard in France, and finally, fleeing "the horrifying facts of life," found peace as an ambulance driver during World War I. All this could be made convincing, but simply dishing it up almost as an afterthought merely confuses things.

Nothing Like Leather, then, is more crisply written and better plotted than its predecessors, but its characters are not fully realized. The plot is absorbing enough to hold a reader's interest, but the ending, in which Burkle drowns in a tanning pit, is more ludicrous than pathetic.[3] Two of England's leading reviewers of the time, Peter Quennell[4] and Derek Verschoyle,[5] praised the book very highly, but readers today would more likely side with the anonymous critic who noted that "his psychological insight seems to imply profundity yet he leaves us puzzled and dissatisfied."[6]

Dead Man Leading

Dead Man Leading (1937) is Pritchett's most ambitious novel, a strenuous and systematic attempt to explore the psychological and moral complexities of his major characters. When the book opens, two explorers named Henry Johnson and Gilbert Phillips are steaming up a dirty Brazilian river toward a rendezvous with their leader, Charles Wright. Johnson falls severely ill with a fever caused partly by his obsessive guilt over a recent love affair with Wright's step-

daughter Lucy Mommbrekke. She was the seducer, but Johnson's puritanical conscience and his groundless fear that she is pregnant
torture him, recalling aspects of *Nothing Like Leather*. Johnson recovers at the expedition's base, the home of a man named Calcott, where
he comes to believe that he has reached a turning point in his life.
"He had passed a crisis. He had begun a new road."[7] When Wright
and Phillips leave briefly, Johnson takes his new canvas boat and
heads upriver, accompanied only by a fantastic Portuguese named
Silva. He intends only to test the boat, but the farther upstream he
travels, the more he becomes obsessed with the idea of tracking down
his father, a missionary who had disappeared in the jungle seventeen
years earlier after leaving Calcott's house and traveling up the same
river. Several days later Johnson and Silva are overtaken by Wright
and Phillips. They persuade Johnson to rejoin the expedition, but
during a hunting foray Wright is accidentally killed. Wright's death
cancels the original expedition but confirms Johnson's resolve to lo-
cate his father, or at least evidence of him. Conscience-stricken by his
own affair with Lucy and unwilling to let Johnson go by himself,
Phillips reluctantly joins him, although he is ill prepared by experience and constitution to undertake such a foolhardy expedition. Phillips and Johnson continue as far as they can by boat and then begin an
arduous trek over land through uncharted scrub country. The longer
the journey proceeds, the more maniacal and senseless it becomes.
Johnson's father in their imaginations grows to something like a god,
and their quest assumes moral and theological dimensions. Johnson
seeks not only his father but also a return of his courage and luck,
while Phillips sees this as a chance to prove himself Johnson's equal
in courage and endurance. Lack of water is their primary danger, and
for several days they stumble through the bush quarreling over
whether to move ahead or to concentrate on finding water. When
they have reached the limits of endurance, Johnson leaves Phillips
near a cave and walks into the jungle. He is never heard of again.
Phillips is saved, first by a rainstorm and then by German traders,
whose cooking fire Phillips mistakes for Johnson's signal. The story
ends with Phillips back in England, talking to Lucy, who has married
in an attempt to erase Johnson's memory.

    Dead Man Leading resembles Conrad's *Heart of Darkness* in setting
and structure, though Pritchett's thematic interests are different.
Both stories involve a journey upriver in search of an elusive and mysterious figure of potent moral force; both treat their respective conti-

nents as uncharted territory resembling the confused, unknown regions of the psyche; and both end in European capitals with a third party interpreting events to a female, who is in neither case told the truth about her man. Atmospheric and tonal similarities also resound, for Pritchett's South America, like Conrad's Africa, is racked by squalor and misery, European exploitation, and moral chaos.

Despite the strangeness of its setting and its radical departure from Pritchett's usual subject matter, *Dead Man Leading* resembles his other novels in two important respects—the dominance of the father figure and the strain of puritanism in the protagonist. Like the author, Harry Johnson has never overcome his father's influence:

He was an open door for [Harry and his two brothers]. They had vision through him. As they had grown up and had become restive in argument with their mother, ripening as she dried up, seeing now a pathos in her narrow energies and opinions, each had privately, unknown to the others, imagined the father—added imagination to what memory there was. Slowly each became not only himself, but the father to himself, in his own fashion. They were themelves and then, added to themselves, some vision seen through the open door. And Harry was the most patient, the most sober and serene of them, Lucy felt. When she left the house that afternoon it was with the feeling that in him the last door of all was this one of his father. (36)

There are other similarities between hero and author: Harry Johnson is one of four children; his mother is flighty and imaginative; religion is important in the family, with the father leading in this as in all things. Late in the book Johnson recalls the last time he saw his father in words that echo *A Cab at the Door*: "They, the children, were excited. They were glad that their father was going because it made them proud and because they would be free" (209). Psychologically, then, Harry Johnson resembles his creator, but physically he is modeled on an unnamed friend of Pritchett's: "I have some stoicism, but I have often thought lately of a courageous friend of mine, now dead, an adventurous explorer, mountaineer and rather reckless yachtsman. He was one of those born to test his fears. I once sailed in a wild gale with him—much against my will—and was terrified, for I am afraid of the sea and have never learned to swim more than 10 yards. He was not afraid. Or, if he feared, his fears exhilarated him. . . ."[8] The sailing episode is recorded in detail in *Dead Man Leading,* only the frightened one is Lucy.

Like so many of Pritchett's male protagonists, Harry Johnson is a puritan. Guilt over Lucy leads to physical illness, which in turn engenders doubt about his courage; for women, as Wright says, "take a man's nerve" (60). Before the affair, Johnson was confident that "Rich or poor, he would have this fine golden wire of luck in his life, the one string that would not snap" (47). Confused feelings increase his guilt and intensify his need to suffer, for now that the flesh has fallen he must punish himself and, if possible, reclaim his innocence—hence the futile search for his father. The novel's action parallels this moral and psychological pilgrimage. As Johnson leaves behind the complexities of civilization, he plunges into the wilderness of his own confused feelings, gradually sloughing off the trappings of civilization until ultimately he strides alone and unencumbered into the jungle. Suffering purifies his soul, and, like his father, he does not die but mysteriously disappears, in his turn becoming the object of speculation and rumor.

The mysteries surrounding Harry Johnson and his father contribute to the novel's complexity. As Conrad invests all events in his story with an air of uncertainty by filtering them through Marlow, so Pritchett's narrator complicates matters by writing his book ostensibly to supersede previous conflicting accounts of Johnson's story. As the novel progresses, there are numerous references to the controversy and to various accounts of the expedition. This device creates a sense of authenticity and reinforces the parallels between father and son, thereby intensifying the mystery and giving the novel an ambiguity more satisfying than any neat conclusion. However, these various accounts also cause an irreconcilable conflict in the point of view. On the one hand, readers are asked to consider the various incomplete versions of the Johnsons' mysteries, but, on the other hand, they must accept Pritchett's resolution of these conflicting stories. Conrad's Marlow is a consistently ambiguous narrator; Pritchett tries to have both mystery and certainty by playing off the false accounts against his own presumably accurate one. In trying to have it both ways, he fully exploits the possibilities of neither.

Among the novel's other characters Gilbert Phillips emerges as second in interest only to Johnson. In the opening chapters Phillips's role is small, but as the novel progresses, he becomes increasingly complex and fascinating, a worthy companion to the confused and driven Johnson. Wright is a bit of stiff cardboard, and Lucy plays too minor a part to develop as a character, but Calcott and Silva are among Pritchett's brilliant minor caricatures. Silva has vitality and a sprightly imagination that sometimes brings him closer to the truth than those who rely prudently on facts. Calcott, by contrast, is a sensualist and reverse snob. Drunken, violent, unscrupulous, and sentimental, he is the moral reflection of the jungle.

These are the various elements that Pritchett brings together in an unusual combination. Not surprisingly, reviewers were sharply divided over the book, in part because its fusion of genres makes it hard to assess. The reviewer for the *Spectator* found it "a rich, a deeply-assimilated, original and satisfying book,"[9] while the *Times Literary Supplement* dismissed all but the chapters dealing with Johnson's trek through the jungle, saying "no amount of imagination can deal with the man's emotional weaknesses, which merely irritate when they should be interesting."[10] Readers looking for adventure will find the novel singularly lacking in heroism, while those expecting psychological insights may find Pritchett's explicit analysis too much like a case study and too little like fiction. It is perhaps on this technical level more than on any other that the novel falters, for Pritchett is so intent on telling us what his character is thinking and feeling that we can follow his decline into madness through a series of all too clearly delineated stages. Harry Johnson is conceived mechanically rather than imaginatively; instead of being revealed indirectly by what he says or does, he is explained in a series of expository passages that leave little for the reader's imagination to work upon.

Pritchett compensates for the inadequacy of his psychological technique in part by his mastery of narrative form. Although structurally the novel resembles a simple journey, events are presented as a mosaic of incidents. Manipulating multiple points of view is part of this technique, and in addition Pritchett skillfully uses flashback and recollection to break the story into a series of episodes. Through these the plot steadily advances, and this gradual process of revelation creates the illusion of dynamic and developing characters. A similar sleight of hand operates in the jungle-adventure portions of the book. The Brazilian forest is made to order for an exciting tale like Haggard's *King Solomon's Mines,* but its dangers, although frequently mentioned, are muted. The only obstacles Johnson and Phillips encounter are the immensity of the land and the shortage of water. These provide excitement without interfering with the psychological tests the two men endure. The only violent death occurs in a stupid accident of the sort that could happen during a grouse hunt, but Pritchett renders the event exciting by his description of Johnson's panic and by the sinister atmosphere of the darkening jungle as it closes in on the two men. Similarly, when Johnson and Phillips are plodding through the scrub in futile pursuit of Johnson's father, Pritchett downplays their sufferings so that he can emphasize the conflicts between them. The most horrifying aspect of their journey is not what happens to their bodies but what occurs to their minds:

The talk was reduced to single words. And those words soon lost their original meanings and new, ridiculous ones or abbreviations were used. . . . Water was called mud. Farina was called sawdust and became abbreviated to "dust." The tough, stringy game was extravagantly called peacock at first but soon became "peek" "pekinese" and finally "dog" when being eaten. The compass was "the jigger." So "take a jig" was to take bearings. Climbing a tree to reconnoitre was turned into "comb the place for lice." Quinine, though never taken, was called gin. Shooting a bird was "balling up a hen" and was reduced to "balling." Phillips made malicious reference to Johnson's Greenland adventure [in which sled dogs had been killed for food] by saying: "What about balling one of the dogs." Enquiries about personal health became obscene. Phillips' diary was his "toilet roll." (203)

There is more genuine horror in this warping of language than in the usual trappings of adventure stories. Paradoxically, focusing on the dynamics between the characters intensifies the physical dangers. This may help to explain why some reviewers were perplexed by the novel's conventional—some said hackneyed—setting and plot. In fact, Pritchett's handling of his materials is highly original.

In spite of its originality *Dead Man Leading* is not the major novel Pritchett intended. At the heart of its failure lies a lack of imaginative grasp of character. Johnson might have become a powerful embodiment of the moral and psychological confusions of modern man, but he fails to seize the imagination because he is presented too much as a prepared specimen, pinned and wriggling. His strivings become eccentricities rather than glorious madness, and in the end he has little to tell us about ourselves. Nevertheless, if *Dead Man Leading* is not a great novel, it is still a very good one. In it Pritchett shows himself a master of narrative form, while at the same time his style has become lean and clear. The creative energy that used to manifest itself in straining after effects has been channeled into controlled description, precise sentences, and evocative imagery. There is only a trace of the old style in the opening pages where Pritchett labors in attempting to convey the oppressiveness of the jungle. However, this mannerism is soon dropped, and the novel as a whole is admirably written. This suggests that with more practice and tenacity Pritchett might have become a major novelist as well as an important short story writer, but fourteen years passed before he produced another novel.

You Make Your Own Life and Other Stories

The 1930s mark the height of Pritchett's period of experiment and development as a fiction writer. The three novels show an ever-increasing mastery of form, and there is parallel development in the short story. *The Spanish Virgin* is largely apprentice work, whereas *You Make Your Own Life* (1938), although uneven in quality, is clearly the work of a more mature, skilled, and confident writer, who continued to experiment with form. The collection contains a variety of stories differing in length, style, subject, narrative technique, and theme. Among the minor pieces, for instance, are "Miss Baker," a tour de force about a schizophrenic woman; "The Upright Man," an antiwar parable almost biblical in style; "Eleven O'Clock," an amusing sketch about infidelity; and "Main Road," a bitter criticism of the pain and dislocation caused by the depression. "X-Ray" captures the essence of institutional coldness by simply describing the contrast between patients' worries and the impersonal surroundings and indifferent staff of a large hospital. "The Aristocrat" is pure Pritchett: a dapper, trim old gentleman enters a pub, engages the regulars in conversation, and does a few magic tricks, one of which wins a sixpence from the pompous Mr. Murgatroyd. When he leaves, the patrons feel sorry for him because they assume that he needed the sixpence to buy his dinner—until Mr. Murgatroyd discovers that his watch is missing. "The Evils of Spain" employs a different kind of comedy by depicting a chaotic group of Spanish men trying to order a meal while they talk over old times. In the end the waiter has to take charge and bring them food and wine, as consensus among them is impossible. As a parable about the political problems of Spain and the Spanish national character, it is very clever.

"The Scapegoat" is more problematic. It begins as a comic tale about the rivalry between two London neighborhoods. Years before Earl Street had broken all records by raising thirty-two pounds to throw a party in honor of a Victoria Cross soldier returning home from World War I. Terence Street is determined to match or exceed this fund for the George V Jubilee (1935); the problem is who to entrust with so large a sum. The neighbors finally choose inconspicuous Art Edwards, and soon the money is piling up. Responsibility brings out the best in Edwards; he becomes outgoing, confident, cheerful, but it also arouses "a curious longing for ups and downs."[11] He takes the entire fund and loses it at the dog track. The outraged neighbors find him dead, a suicide by hanging. When Earl Street jeers, there is a fierce fight, and then Terence Street gives Edwards the biggest funeral the neighborhood has ever seen. The tragicomic nature of this story is part of its puzzling quality, further complicated by its overtones of political allegory: "The truth is that you can't live without enemies and the best enemies are the ones nearest home . . ." (189). Since the story first appeared in the *London Mercury* in 1937, when rumblings of war were already audible, it seems likely that Pritchett intended a political message, although exactly what message he had in mind is unclear. He has never chosen "The Scapegoat" for inclusion in any of his collected volumes, but the story may have more staying power than he suspects, for it resonates in the mind and teases one's curiosity.

"Page and Monarch" moves us from the neighborhoods of London's working class to the upper echelons of the middle class. Thematically, it echoes some of the concerns of *Nothing Like Leather,* while in its characters and situations it looks forward to "The Chain-Smoker" (1969) and "The Last Throw" (1974). The chief figure in the story is Lippott, assistant to a retail tycoon named Schneider, for whom he has worked many years, rising from poverty to a salary of three thousand pounds. Schneider is the monarch, a man who owns things and people, moving like a renaissance prince from city to city, mistresses trailing, secretaries hovering, servants groveling, Rolls Royce purring. Lippott is largely responsible for the firm's daily operations, but he remains insignificant beside his boss, little more than an upstart clerk in expensive suits.

On the day of the story Schneider has left London for a holiday in Paris; the Christmas rush is over, and there is time to relax until spring. Having little to do, Lippott takes a walk. He enters a piano store and asks for Mrs. Cambery, a competent, polished, well-dressed woman in her late forties who is Schneider's ex-mistress. Schneider had once offered her to Lippott. Lippott inquires about gramophones, and as she demonstrates them he considers why she is there and how similar they are—climbers who capitalized on an opportunity provided by Schneider—though Lippott considers himself superior. She plays a recording of "Good King Wenceslas," and suddenly Lippott sees in the carol his own origins, the poor man gathering fuel, invited to dine by the good king: "Page and Monarch forth they went / Forth they went together" (250). He buys the gramophone and walks back to his office. Entering the building, he sees a number of young men standing around the elevator, idle. Thinking of the 120 guineas he spent on the gramophone and that "Schneider must be paid for" (253), he orders three of the elevator men fired—a week before Christmas.

"Page and Monarch" is a story about power, the power of Schneider to raise Lippott from a lowly clerk to a highly paid assistant, to take on and discard mistresses at will, to sign huge contracts and thereby to demand respect, and to "give away" another human being. Lippott has power of his own. Unlike King Wenceslas, however, he uses his power destructively, mainly because he resents being so completely under Schneider's control. Listening to the various gramophones, he realized that, "The sound of music meant to him the spending of money. One could reckon up the price per bar, bill totals by the top notes" (248). However, "Good King Wenceslas" reminds him of an alternative set of values, beyond power and money. Having denied himself amusements, family connections, and love, he cannot bear to consider that he has chosen unwisely, so he fires the men to "pay" Schneider. He is not merely the monarch's page; he is his fool.

"You Make Your Own Life" is one of Pritchett's best. On the surface it seems a casual, effortless, and inconsequential story within a story. The narrator of the frame tale, waiting for a train in a provincial town, decides to have his hair cut. When he climbs into the chair, the barber begins to talk about the previous customer, a lifelong friend who once suffered from tuberculosis. During his illness the barber's fiancée visited him, and he fell in love with her. So determined was he to have the girl that he tried to kill the barber with poisoned whiskey and, failing at this, slit his own throat as a wedding "present" for the bride. Since then, the barber has been shaving him every day. The customer visits Sundays to play with the barber's children and goes out with different girls nearly every week. " 'It's a dead place, this, all right in the summer on the river. You make your own life' " (277).

Part of the effect of this story is the droll, understated way it is told. The barber relates it matter-of-factly, without the slightest trace of emotion, yet this is the stuff of melodrama—tuberculosis, thwarted love, attempted murder, and suicide. A popular novelist would spin a plot of five hundred pages around the events Pritchett reduces to a few casual paragraphs. Presenting the story in this way, Pritchett risks trivializing it, for such tales are as old as David and Bathsheba and as new as the tabloid the narrator reads while waiting his turn. For the barber it is personal and perhaps rather boring; the important thing is that he married the prettiest girl in town and managed to keep his best friend alive. To us it is a remarkable narrative about the elasticity of human nature and the surprises of poetic justice.

"The Two Brothers" recasts the Cain and Abel myth as a modern tale of psychological conflict. Like their biblical originals, the two brothers are so unlike as hardly to seem related. Micky, also known as the Yank because he lived for a time in Canada, is energetic, decisive, and domineering; Charlie is now ill, weak, vacillating, and declining into madness, although at one time he held a promising job in a bank. The brothers have been reunited after World War I, in which Micky fought on the British side, and this is the cause of Charlie's problem, for in a small Irish town such a brother is more than an embarrassment: others in this situation had been threatened or murdered, and Charlie has received a hate letter. Micky returned from the war to find his clever brother reduced to a bundle of fears, and for three years he has been caring for him, easing him out of hospitals into a rest home, and finally to a drafty, tumbledown house near the Atlantic, where Micky can ramble gun in hand over the dunes, enjoying the wide spaces until his return to Canada. Micky's departure is Charlie's ultimate fear, and when it happens, Charlie's decline is swift. Living in gale-swept isolation with the tatters of his past, he becomes gaunt and withdrawn. Accusing memories haunt him. Racked by horrid dreams and pursued by fear and some hinted-at but nameless guilt, Charlie commits suicide.

"The Two Brothers" is a bleak and powerful story, comparable in tone and impact to H. E. Bates's "The Mill" and A. E. Coppard's "The Higgler." Every element contributes to the sense of helplessness and isolation that drives Charlie to suicide. The atmosphere of the sea-lashed coast, the bare ruin of the house and its wild garden, the fears and desperation of Charlie's memories and imagination combine to produce a chilling tale of madness and death. Along with the mystery of Charlie's madness is the question Cain asked of God, "Am I my brother's keeper?" The economy required by the short story has eliminated the excessive explanation that plagued *Dead Man Leading* and has disciplined Pritchett's style into taut, clear, suggestive writing. The dialogue is racy and believable, the structure highly controlled, and the characterizations strong and detailed. "The Two Brothers" is not a typical Pritchett story, but it is among his most memorable.

The longest and most ambitious story of *You Make Your Own Life* is "Handsome Is as Handsome Does," concerning a middle-aged couple united against a world that humiliates and rejects them. At the center is Mrs. Coram, whom Pritchett describes very unflatteringly as ugly and "rat-like, with that peculiar busyness, inquisitiveness, intelligence and even charm of rats" (71). Born into the poor gentry, she was expected to marry an army officer and settle down to a life of organized boredom, but she rejected her class and married a chemical engineer from a grimy working-class town. He is unlike her in all respects except that he too is ugly. Thick, dull-witted, slow of speech, crude, uneducated, and unmannerly, he quarrels constantly with everyone. She is his interpreter and shield, translating his inarticulate mumblings, smoothing over his rudeness, and apologizing for his ill manners and lack of tact. Even as she protects him, however, he accuses her of "getting at him." Emotionally he is still in the acidic streets of Leicester, clawing his way by scholarships and hard work to his present position, where he now has no hope of advancement. Their common tragedy is that they are childless.

The story is set on the French Mediterranean, where they are taking their first holiday abroad. Coram regards the beautiful scenery and the cheery hotel proprietor as frauds, while the appearance of a handsome young man named Alex reminds Mrs. Coram of the son she never had. The story reaches its climax when M. Pierre (the hotel proprietor), Alex, and the Corams go to a beach, where the water is rough and the undertow dangerous. The undertow pulls M. Pierre out to sea and would drown him except for a daring rescue by Alex, a feat that Coram could not even think of performing. For the first time Mrs. Coram turns against her husband, isolating him in his speechless humiliation. That evening M. Pierre characteristically brags about nearly drowning, neglecting to mention Alex's heroism, while Mrs. Coram tells the story to some new English arrivals—making her husband the hero. Once more it is "The Corams against the world" (134).

This is the kind of material upon which Pritchett's imagination works most effectively. The Corams are ugly, almost repulsive people, yet Pritchett takes us inside their lives and forces us to see that they are deeply wounded and deserving of sympathy. By contrast, the ebullient M. Pierre is shallow and trite, complacent in his self-centeredness. Alex wears the protective oil of youth. The Corams have only each other, and although in many ways their lives are grotesque, they are genuine people, thwarted, unhappy, uncouth, but entirely human.

But of the items in this collection "Sense of Humour" most clearly proclaims Pritchett's maturity as a short story writer. This story haunts the mind and disturbs the conscience, as Pritchett peels back the layers of middle-class hypocrisy with such tact and precision that we are more fascinated than horrified by what we see. The narrator and central character is Arthur Humphrey, a traveling salesman who meets Muriel MacFarlane, a hotel clerk, during his first trip into his new territory. She is dating Colin Mitchell, a local boy who rides a motorcycle and is very much in love with her, but Humphrey soon replaces Colin in Muriel's affections. Although Muriel has never taken Colin seriously, he cannot give her up and begins to follow the couple everywhere they go. Humphrey is annoyed but tries to remain friendly:

I felt sorry for that fellow. He knew it was hopeless, but he loved her. I suppose he couldn't help himself. . . . He couldn't save money, so he lost her. I suppose all he thought of was love.

I could have been friends with that fellow. As it was, I put a lot of business his way. I didn't want him to get the wrong idea about me. We're all human after all. (20)

When a holiday comes around and they want to visit Humphrey's parents, Colin tries to ruin their plans by saying he cannot repair Humphrey's car, so they are forced to go by train. Shortly after they arrive, Muriel receives a call from the police: Colin has been killed in a motorcycle accident while pursuing her. His body is brought to the Humphrey home because Arthur's father is an undertaker. Muriel is distraught at his death and goes to bed, crying and whispering Colin's name over and over. Arthur sits by her side, trying to comfort her, his mind wandering from his company's new line of goods to Colin's accident. After a while, he lies down beside her:

This Colin thing seemed to have knocked the bottom out of everything and I had a funny feeling we were going down and down and down in a lift. And the further we went, the hotter and softer she got. Perhaps it was when I found with my hands that she had very big breasts. But it was like being on the mail steamer and feeling engines start under your feet, thumping louder and louder. You can feel it in every vein of your body. Her mouth opened and her tears dried. Her breath came through her open mouth and her voice was blind and husky. Colin, Colin, Colin, she said, and her fingers were hooked into me. I got out and turned the key in the door. (28)

For practical reasons, they decide to return Colin's body to his home town with Humphrey driving the hearse and Muriel riding with him. As they do so, Colin follows them for the last time in the coffin in the back of the hearse. When they pass through a town, people pause or raise their hats in honor of the deceased. They feel honored, like royalty. "I was proud of her, I was proud of Colin, and I was proud of myself. And after what had happened, I mean on the last two nights, it was like a wedding. And although we knew it was for Colin, it was for us too, because Colin was with both of us. It was like this all the way. 'Look at that man there. Why doesn't he raise his hat? People ought to show respect for the dead,' she said" (37).

Pritchett's handling of this unusual, and at times grotesque, material is brilliant. So sure is his control that he poises the reader on a knife's edge between laughter and tears, loathing and sympathy. He accomplishes this by making Humphrey a naive narrator, telling us reliably what happened but unaware of the multiple ironies of his words and actions. He is not smug, but morally obtuse, his soul a double-entry ledger, yet he is saved from caricature by the tone of questioning that pervades the story. Clearly there is much he does not understand; in particular, he will never know whether Murial makes love to him or to her memory of Colin, nor will he ever know whether she married him for himself or for his money and mobility. Muriel is equally complex and intriguing. Several times she accounts for her behavior by saying, "I'm Irish. I've got a sense of humour," which to her means that she can laugh at herself and the absurdities of human folly; it also suggests that she can brush aside suffering.

The one person who genuinely loves is the inarticulate Colin, able to express his feelings only by the annoying habit of following Muriel and Arthur. Sadly, he wins Muriel's affections only after he dies. In this story Pritchett first learns to exploit and control multiple layers of subtle irony and grim humor, the qualities that set his stories apart and mark them with his individual stamp. Incidentally, he originally titled this story "The Commercial Traveller" but changed it at the suggestion of John Lehmann, editor of *New Writing,* where it first appeared because the higher-paying magazines rejected it.[12] Fittingly it marks Pritchett's maturity as a short story writer and a man with a sense of humor.

The stories collected in *You Make Your Own Life* and those published during the thirties in various magazines show Pritchett experimenting with a variety of methods. "The Chimney" (*New Statesman,* 26 December 1936) is a rural sketch of atmosphere and character, while at the other extreme is the Kafkaesque psychological horror of "Miss Baker." "Main Road" protests against economic and social injustice, but "In Autumn Quietly" (*John 'o London's Weekly,* 4 February 1933) resembles the contrived ironies of an O. Henry story. Clearly, however, Pritchett was developing his own material and style, finding his métier in sympathetically satirical portraits of the urban middle class. What evolved was wholly his own, though inspired by Arnold Bennett and H. G. Wells in its subject and indebted to Turgenev and Maupassant for the polish and precision of its style. His characters have been compared in their eccentricity with those of Dickens, though without the sentimentality and verbosity. Pritchett's unique blend of matter and manner sets him apart from other short story writers of the thirties; only Sylvia Townsend Warner resembles him, and then only in her less fantastic, more realistic moods.[13] The best of Pritchett's short fiction in this period incorporates his intimate knowledge of the lower middle classes with his wide reading in French and Russian fiction to produce stories that stand apart, like their author, from the literary and intellectual mainstream. This is why Pritchett remained a writer's writer, admired by contemporaries like Richard Church, Gerald Brenan, and John Lehmann, but otherwise quite isolated from the literary life of his time.

Chapter Four
War Years and After

World War II ended what has been called the golden age of the British short story, marking the close of a literary renaissance that had begun about 1910, a period that John Holloway compares in achievement with the ages of Shakespeare (1590–1612), Swift (1710–1735), and Wordsworth (1793–1822).[1] This was also the last time when literature dominated British culture. After the war the basic structures of a scientific and technological culture were firmly in place. The new would have replaced the old in any event, but the war hastened its advance and simultaneously disrupted the career of nearly every author in the country. Fortunately, officials were determined to avoid the mistakes of World War I, when many of England's most promising young men were killed at the front, and so most writers drafted into the military were given noncombat assignments where they could serve by using their talents. For a few writers national service was the making of their careers (H. E. Bates and William Sansom come to mind), but for the majority, Pritchett included, the war was an interruption at best, as indicated by the fact that he produced only a collection of critical essays and a few stories during the war.

It May Never Happen

It May Never Happen (1945) is a transitional collection, marking the end of Pritchett's apprenticeship as a story writer and the beginning of his maturity. Although none of the stories lacks merit, the majority are accomplished without being distinguished, while a few are below his standard and at least two are classics. The weaker stories include three connected with the war: "The Ape," a thin and somewhat forced political allegory; "The Voice," the tale of a reprobate Welsh clergyman trapped in a bombed church; and "The Lion's Den," a fictional treatment of Pritchett's parents that emphasizes Walter Pritchett's irrational need to hoard and guard material possessions. The collection also includes a large group of autobiographical stories, covering various periods in Pritchett's life. "The Night

63

Worker" and "Aunt Gertrude" derive from his childhood and hold more than passing interest as evocations of a boy's outlook on the world and his growing awareness of adult life. "The Chestnut Tree," "The Clerk's Tale," and "It May Never Happen" feature Pritchett as a young clerk in the leather trade or furniture business, struggling chiefly with problems of sexuality. From these emerges a portrait of the author as a young puritan, separating the spirit and flesh in an attempt to idealize his sexual feelings. In "The Chestnut Tree," for example, the young man is reprimanded by the chief clerk for his attentions to the younger of two sisters working in the office. At the chief clerk's side he hears at close range the perpetual "Um, Um, Um" that sounds like "the neural, aimless, mindless rumble of the ape digesting its inexplicable years on earth."[2] These rumblings are the growling of a beast: "The spirit and the flesh turned a somersault inside me. . . . the flesh triumphed. I hated Hester Browne, I saw the deadly nightshade under her eyes. . ." (145). For the young protagonists of Pritchett's stories, physical passion is bestial; its symbol is the ape.

We know from Pritchett's autobiography and his private letters that he was nearly obsessed by questions of sexuality and the complexities of the father-son relationship. One of the most successful stories to deal with the latter problem is "The Fly in the Ointment," which thinly disguises Walter Pritchett as a bankrupt businessman and the author as his son, Harold. Although Harold has come to offer comfort and support, he and his father soon bicker, as father criticizes him for failing to think big and Harold retorts that big ideas have led his father to catastrophe. They are saved from an outright quarrel by a buzzing fly that the father insists must be killed, and for a moment they cooperate in this trivial distraction, emblematic of the barriers that have come between them over the years and of the father's elusive goals. The fly escapes, but the effort leaves the old man feeling dizzy. For a moment, mutual concerns about age and health bring father and son as close as they can come to real affection. Then, inevitably, father launches into one of his set speeches. He was wrong to pursue money. The Israelites did not seek wealth but merely collected manna. What he wants now is a cottage by the sea, though he has no means of procuring it. Awkwardly, Harold suggests that perhaps he could raise a little cash. " 'Raise it?' said the old man sharply. 'Why didn't you tell me before you could raise money? How can you raise it? Where? By when?' " (176). In this instant the story becomes comic, and the better we know Walter Pritchett, the more amusing the joke. Yet to regard the story simply as a satiric portrait of an old man unable to be truthful with himself would be to miss the point, for the relationship between father and son is complex and dynamic. Harold is almost pathetic in his caution and lack of imagination. The old man at least has vitality, although it is the energy of a snake oil salesman. Here, then, is the history of a father and son, crystallized into a few moments in an empty factory. Both the setting and the appearance of the fly remind us of Katherine Mansfield's story "The Fly," for both stories use the symbol with similar tact and poignancy. Pritchett's story, while less heartrending, is more emotionally complex, comedy adding a unique kind of pain to this portrait of multiple failure and Pritchett's generous spirit making his father not an object of scorn but of sorrow.

Two other stories illustrate aspects of Pritchett's maturing art. "Many Are Disappointed" is a sketch in the 1930s English manner, derived from Chekhov, of presenting a brief and apparently trivial moment as suggestive of more significant patterns of action. Four young men on a cycling tour of England's Roman roads have been traveling all morning and are anticipating a stop at a pub. Instead, they find only a house, a timid woman who sells tea, and a meager fare of bread and tomatoes. "Many are disappointed," she admits. After tea one of the four discovers that she is among the disappointed, having come to this remote place for her husband's health only to find loneliness and financial troubles. When the four leave, the three unmarried men again hope for a pub with a pretty barmaid, a good steak, and a hearty glass of beer. Only Ted, the married man, has no expectations, and the story suggests that the others will eventually learn the same lesson. Brief sketches of this type that rely on indirection and implication test an author's sense of form and his powers of suggestion and economy. Pritchett passes these tests, demonstrating the craftsman's ability to crowd a great deal onto a small canvas.

"Pocock Passes" exhibits an equally subtle and complex artistry in presenting an unusual character of elusive significance. The story begins and ends with Mr. Rogers contemplating the death of his friend, Mr. Pocock, whom he knew for only a few months. Drawn together by obesity and love of drink, they meet nightly in the lounge bar, at first like "two dogs," later like "lovers" (89). Pocock claims to be a London painter, intimate with the art world, although he never seems to work; similarly, Rogers has retired from real estate to concentrate on food and alcohol. The highlight of their friendship is an excursion to a nearby town for a night of theater and drinking, which they finish in Pocock's shockingly messy cottage where Rogers for the first time sees Pocock's paintings, particularly a revolting nude. Shortly afterwards Pocock dies, but two years later Rogers sees him in a detective film, dressed as he had been for their outing in a loud checked suit. The audience roars with laughter at Pocock's ridiculous figure. Knowing now about Pocock's past, Rogers returns home, takes the one painting he had saved, and burns it. "Rogers heard in the husky roar of the flame the sound of a soul set free, all stain removed" (98).

In part this is a story of self-deception, since Pocock is not what he claims to be, but even more so it concerns two men who have cut themselves off from the world through obesity and alcohol. Their gestures of friendship are awkward and befuddled by drink, yet they retain an air of dignity by the calm with which they accept isolation and ruin. Stylistically the story reflects the disorder of the characters' lives. Conversations are jerky and cryptic, and events are loosely connected, as if drifting toward misfortune. Beneath their exterior calm and their layers of protective fat, however, lies the fear of death, the final loneliness that awaits everyone, movingly portrayed in Pocock's delirious banging with his cane on the cottage floor, calling for help. He is an archetypal figure of age, knocking on the earth like the mysterious stranger in Chaucer's "Pardoner's Tale" for entrance to a grave. Rogers perceives that he will follow Pocock to the same end, "living on his capital like his friend." "Pocock Passes" is typical of Pritchett in presenting multiple ironies about unpleasant people while still managing to win the reader's sympathy for them. In these lonely, drunken figures he touches a core of humanity.

The acknowledged classics of this collection and the stories that undeniably marked Pritchett's entrance into the front rank of short story writers of his generation are "The Saint" and "The Sailor." In "The Saint" it is easy to recognize autobiographical material used in other stories—the boy, his uncle, and the Purification Church of Toronto. The plot itself is summarized in the opening sentence, "When I was seventeen years old I lost my religious faith. It had been unsteady for some time and then, very suddenly, it went as the result of an incident in a punt on the river outside the town where we lived" (37). The boy's doubts center on the origin of evil, which he imagines as an ape. If evil is an illusion, he asks, where does the illusion originate? He remains poised between faith and doubt until Mr. Timberlake arrives for a visit. So impressive is the minister from Toronto that the boy's doubts evaporate, but Mr. Timberlake has been fore-warned of the young man's problems and insists on taking him out in a punt to have a talk about evil. The accident as Pritchett describes it is both funny and sad. Ignoring the boy's advice, Timberlake takes the punt under a willow tree and ends up hanging from one of its branches, slowly sinking into the water. What the boy sees as Timberlake dangles from the branch is strangely significant, for as he slowly sinks his shirt pulls out of his trousers, revealing a patch of pale skin like a crack in the statue of a Greek god. At that moment the boy sees that Mr. Timberlake knows nothing about the origin of evil.

The statue image indicates that the boy sees not only Mr. Timberlake's humanity but also his pretenses. The expression of sadness on his face, the signs of "deprecation and pathos" (47) prove that the man is maintaining a front. For the rest of the outing, in fact, he pretends that nothing has happened. They continue upriver and rest a while in a buttercup meadow; even when Timberlake's suit becomes coated in pollen so that he resembles a gilded statue, he acknowledges nothing. Thus the boy comes to see that Timberlake has no interest in the world and is bored by it. "He was a dull man, duller than any man I have ever known; but his dullness was a sort of earthly deposit left by a being whose diluted mind was far away in the effervescence of metaphysical matters" (49). The phrase "earthly deposit," like the "gross ape" that the young man associates with his doubts, suggests the reality of the material world, the flesh beneath the pant-loops and brace-tabs, those artificial devices that hide the ape under the clothes. There is an almost exact parallel in *Mr. Beluncle,* when the young man of that novel is listening to a preacher like Mr. Timberlake. Trying to attend to the sermon, his mind involuntarily conjures an extraordinary vision:

And then, a terrible thing happened. Henry's faith went. Henry's fancy un-buttoned Mr. Van der Hoek's trousers from their braces. Slowly he lowered them, crumpling their creases. He pulled Mr. Van der Hoek's trousers down to his ankles. He removed his underpants. Fighting with all his might against the impulse, he exposed the mild and thoughtful private organs of the lecturer.[3]

The link between sexuality and the ape beneath the clothes is a recurring motif in Pritchett's fiction and is related to those stories in which the protagonist struggles with the flesh and spirit. The origin of evil is linked in Pritchett's mind with man's animality, his sexuality in particular. In a letter to Gerald Brenan he once remarked that while he did not believe in the Fall he did accept the idea of Original Sin (2 February 1944).

The autobiographical sidelights help explain why "The Saint" ends as it does. Years later the narrator learns of Mr. Timberlake's death at age fifty-seven, and he reflects on the events of that afternoon. "I understood why he did not talk to me about the origin of evil. He was honest. The ape was with us. The ape that merely followed me was already inside Mr. Timberlake eating out his heart" (51–52). In "The Saint" Pritchett found the perfect vehicle for his theme that the beginning of wisdom lies in accepting humanity, ape and all. The adolescent is appalled and even repelled by the body, physical desire, and mortality; the adult understands and accepts them. Dramatically and symbolically these ideas emerge from "The Saint" where Pritchett affirms "the disasters and beauties of the world" that cannot be denied or wished away. They are the fullness of life. Here Pritchett's characters, story, and tone unite in one of the finest examples of the storyteller's art.

"The Sailor" certainly equals and perhaps even excels "The Saint," yet it is difficult to say just wherein the greatness of "The Sailor" lies, for even after several readings it does not strike one as profound. Like many other great stories, it is so perfectly entertaining that it almost discourages close analysis, not because we fear analysis will diminish the story but because it seems unnecessary. Nevertheless, successive readings only confirm the first impression that this is one of the outstanding stories in the language. Three characters of nearly equal interest occupy our attention, but for several pages we meet only two, the sailor Albert Thompson and the narrator, a professional writer who bears more than a slight resemblance to Pritchett. Indeed, he once confided to Gerald Brenan that Thompson closely resembles a sailor he had once employed (undated letter ca. 1938). The two men meet accidentally in London, when the sailor stops the author to ask directions to Whitechapel, for which he has been searching all day. The writer notices that the poor man is soaking wet, completely out of his element, and incapable of following the simplest directions. The author offers to buy him a drink, but the sailor refuses because it is "temptation." Intrigued by this puritanical response, the author (admittedly a puritan himself) buys the sailor a pot of tea and offers him a job as housekeeper. " 'Thank Gawd I stopped you,' [the sailor says]. 'I kep' stopping people all day and they messed me up, but you been straight' " (2). The sailor's battles with temptation constitute much of the story's dramatic interest, for between him and the writer, who calls himself "a fellow-struggler with sin" (2), there soon develops a contest of wills. Thompson takes the approach suggested by the Lord's Prayer, "Lead me not into temptation," while the author prefers the advice of Mark Twain's "The Man That Corrupted Hadleyburg," "Lead us into temptation." Thus, for the first few weeks Thompson does not venture out of doors, claiming that he cannot do so without becoming lost. He even asks his employer to keep his pay, for that too is temptation.

If the writer offers security and freedom from temptation to the sailor, the sailor in turn brings cleanliness and order. Returning from a morning's walk, the writer sees smoke billowing from his chimney "with such dense streaming energy that the house looked like a destroyer racing full steam ahead into the wave of hills" (7). When he enters, he has an even greater surprise: "I thought I had come into the wrong house. The paint had been scrubbed, the floors polished like decks, the reflections of the firelight danced in them, the windows gleamed, and the room was glittering with polished metal. Door-knobs, keyholes, fire-irons, window-catches, were polished; metal which I had no idea existed flashed with life" (7). Life becomes as punctual and well ordered as a ship at sea, reinforcing the author's idea that "The secret of happiness is to find a congenial monotony" (8). In contrast to the spit and polish of the author's household is the disarray of the bungalow and garden of the story's third character, the colonel's daughter. She lives in moral and physical chaos, the cast-off mistress of a gas-heater salesman, inhabiting a house known in the area for its heap of discarded liquor bottles and its tangled garden. She adds generously to the collection of bottles and digs in the garden only to bury tin cans. She has a "limpid wink" as "enticing as a fish rising" and was "the hardest-drinking and most blasphemous piece of apparent childish innocence you had ever seen" (5–6). She has quickly gained a local reputation for promiscuity, although whether deservedly or not is uncertain, and as the story progresses, she becomes the author's temptation. Before meeting her, he was content without sex, but her suggestive wink, casual manners, candid conversation, and racy suggestiveness are hard to resist. Meanwhile, the author is tempting Thompson, although he thinks of himself as freeing the sailor from unreasonable fears. At first through suggestions and then by orders, he makes Thompson run errands in the village. The results are predictable: he becomes lost and frightens local women by following them in hopes of finding his way back. As he learns the territory, however, everything becomes temptation to him, and far from avoiding it, he begins seeking it out. He stops everyone he sees and talks incessantly about avoiding temptation, often following them wherever they go. In his own mind he never talked to anyone "—it was untrue, but it was not a lie. It was simply a delusion" (16). Temptation climaxes for both men on the same night. The postman invites Thompson to come to the Legion Hall for drinks, and for a whole day he wrestles with the dilemma. When the author leaves that evening, ostensibly for a walk but in fact to find the colonel's daughter, Thompson is safe in the kitchen, reading a western novel. The bungalow, however, is dark, so the writer takes a long walk, and when he returns his house is dark and presumably Thompson has gone to bed. Then the writer hears voices approaching, and in stumble Thompson and the colonel's daughter, both very drunk and she with her skirt awry. Both men have fallen, although the author symbolically rather than literally. From this point on, Thompson spends evenings at the local pub, buying everyone drinks. In the end the author goes to Europe and Thompson returns to London, optimistically certain he will again land on his feet. We last glimpse him plunging into the London traffic in search of Whitechapel.

In "The Sailor" Pritchett shows himself to be the complete master of his comic materials. Everything about the story rings true, in spite of its slightly old-fashioned concern with temptation and its daringly individualized characters. The style is meticulously exact: from its opening description of the sailor walking through the London rain as if "he were breaking through the bead curtain of a Pernambuco bar" (1) to the concluding paragraph in which the sailor takes his leave, there is not a word out of place or in excess. Holding everything together is Pritchett's masterful control of tone, which blends simple sincerity with sophisticated wit. As a result, neither the characters nor the situations ever lose their comic originality, yet in spite of themselves they suggest both the archetypal fall and the rhythm of everyday life. Everything about this story is fresh and original, from its unerringly accurate dialogue to its precise and evocative descriptions.

Equally brilliant is Pritchett's seamless joining of character and idea. The sailor is like many of Pritchett's eccentrics in that he cannot cope with the simplest of life's problems nor follow the most basic of his own precepts, yet we cannot accuse him of stupidity or hypocrisy. He is simply lost in the complexities of the world and handles them best when he retreats into orderly domesticity. Even when he falls, however, he remains innocent. The morning after his debauch with the colonel's daughter, "He behaved as though nothing had happened" (23). She tempted him and he fell—as matter-of-factly as lanes confuse him and London people are not "straight." It is a tribute to Pritchett's controlled style that such a character can simultaneously evoke laughter and sympathy. By contrast, the colonel's daughter lives a disorderly modern life in which words like *temptation* and *sin* have no meaning, even if alcoholic unhappiness does. She is the perfect contrast to the sailor, although like him she retains an air of innocence, a ruined Eve in a weedy garden. Between them is the narrator, pulled on the one hand by the sailor's orderly life of ascetic denial and on the other by temptations of the flesh. For him sinlessness resides in middle-class respectability, in the "congenial monotony" of country life, which is in part only an avoidance of responsibility. In some ways he is the snake, tempting Thompson to conquer his weaknesses while at the same time succumbing to his own. The irony is saved from obviousness or bitterness by Pritchett's sardonic wit and the gentle obtuseness with which he invests his narrator.

The ironies and multiple suggestions of this story are nearly endless, but one that deserves special mention is Pritchett's reversal of the usual town-country dichotomy. The action begins and ends in London, traditionally the Sodom and Gomorrah of England, but the temptations that the characters struggle against are in the remote countryside, the supposedly idyllic refuge from the complexities and immoralities of modern life. It is here, not in the city, that both men fall. The colonel's daughter, the British legion, and the villagers themselves provide all the wickedness either man needs. Returning from the country, the sailor once again goes in search of Whitechapel, surely one of the most effective and unobtrusive symbols ever to grace an English short story.

Mr. Beluncle

The publication of *Dead Man Leading* in 1937 seemed to indicate that Pritchett had overcome most of the stylistic and structural problems of his first three novels and had essentially learned the techniques of novel construction. The fourteen years between *Dead Man Leading* and *Mr. Beluncle* (1951) were filled with the distractions of family, war, and journalism that prevented him from concentrating on a novel. In fact, *Mr. Beluncle* was some ten years in the writing[4] and might never have been completed except for the loan from Gerald Brenan. The wavering structure of the novel shows, however, that Pritchett's difficulties were more technical than psychological, and in the end he himself recognized that the book was not the success he had hoped it would be (VSP to GB postmarked 14 March 1950).

By Pritchett's own admission *Mr. Beluncle* is based almost entirely on autobiographical material. Philip Beluncle is but a thin disguise for Walter Pritchett; Ethel Beluncle is unmistakably Beatrice; the oldest son Henry is Victor as a young man, and the fictional George and Leslie are his two younger brothers, Cyril and Gordon. Mrs. Truslove can probably be equated with Walter's partner, Miss H. The minor characters are less identifiable, although Mr. Beluncle's mother closely resembles Walter's mother as described in the autobiography, and the scandalous Connie may be based on the twice-married Aunt Ada Bugg of Ipswich. *Mr. Beluncle,* therefore, is drawn from the period when Victor was about thirteen or fourteen and his father had entered the relatively prosperous period as a manufacturer of needlework. In the novel, however, Henry is nineteen and working in his father's factory, the time when Victor was actually apprenticed in the leather trade. There is some overlap, therefore, between *Mr. Beluncle* and *Nothing Like Leather,* but the later book contains a far more accurate and satirical portrait of Walter Pritchett and, indeed, of the whole family. In essence, *Mr. Beluncle* is Pritchett's last major attempt to exorcise the ghost of his father and perhaps to take revenge for the humiliations he suffered as a young man.

Describing the plot of *Mr. Beluncle* is difficult, since there is no steadily advancing story line. The first ten chapters are the most coherent and effective, unified by the simple device of tracing the movements and thoughts of Mr. Beluncle and his family from Saturday noon through Sunday night. Pritchett's tone is mocking and irreverent as he describes Beluncle's place of business, delves into his fantastically overactive imagination, and exposes his humbug and pomposity. Along the way we see Henry fight back tears and stand up to his father, vainly striving to maintain the sense of superiority he has gained by reading extensively and mastering French, simultaneously clinging desperately to his adolescent crush on Mary Phibbs.

George tries hopelessly to earn his father's love, while Leslie rises above the family's problems by ridiculing its vanities and pretensions. Along the way, we meet Mary Phibbs's father (who sounds uncannily like Dorothy's father in *Nothing Like Leather*), the religious fanatics Granger and Vogg who despise the Purification Church, Lady Roads (the head of the Purification congregation), Mrs. Truslove and her crippled sister Judy, and a handful of lesser characters. Everything at this point bears the stamp of Dickens and H. G. Wells's *Mr. Polly*, with Beluncle acting like a latter-day Mr. Micawber. A Dickensian love of character and comedy, the smoky presence of commercial and manufacturing London, and a Wellsian air of lower middle-class hypocrisy and nonsense envelope everything and everyone. However, after a promising, even at times brilliant, ten chapters, the novel loses its bearings, and although it is sustained for another hundred pages by the high level of interest Pritchett generates in his characters and by the rich comedy of several scenes, it finally loses momentum and direction and coasts to a stop.

Many of the novel's problems can be ascribed to its uncertainty of purpose. For the first third of the book Pritchett brilliantly exorcises the demons of his father's comic pretensions and religious self-delusion:

The Parkinsonians—their correct name was The Church of the Last Purification, Toronto—were a healthy-looking collection of clean, smiling people, broad and bummy, whether male or female, and, with the exception of one or two poor people among them, they dressed expensively. Among the summer dresses, the fine hats—some of them from Bond Street—and the scents, there sat living examples of prayer promptly answered; and the satisfaction of it seemed, in each case, to have added weight to the person. People who were converted to the Purification put on weight at once, as if it had been sent down to them by the Central Committee of the party. (*B*, 91)

Even richer and more telling is a passage of dialogue recorded during Sunday's dinner:

"When I go to my factory and make furniture, to mortal sense I seem to be making wardrobes, armchairs, and so on, but really I am spreading love." Mr. Beluncle raised his short heavy arms and was himself struck by the luxuriousness of his soft pink hands which seemed to smooth the very air. "And the more I spread love, the more orders I get and it's right for me to have orders because orders are giving love. It is not money we want, it is love."

"What I can't understand," Ethel said, "is why you had such a bad year last year." (B, 91)

When Pritchett has apparently exhausted these aspects of Beluncle, he focuses on the religiosity of the Parkinsonians and the fanaticism of Vogg. Accordingly, he follows Vogg and Granger as they distribute tracts, takes us to a special purification lecture by Mr. Van der Hoek at which Vogg "bears witness" by shouting "Lies!" and "Blasphemy!" in response to the speaker, and then brings these together by making Vogg paradoxically responsible for the miracle of Judy Dyke's cure. Other episodes in this vein include a running battle between two factions of the Purification church, the aftermath of Miss Dykes's healing, and the apostasy of Henry, who realizes the truth of Vogg's accusations and confesses to Mary that he no longer believes. In this scene Henry mentally undresses Van der Hoek as discussed earlier. These episodes form a kind of subtheme to the main action, but they are equally inconclusive and uncertain of purpose. Another idea that could have sustained the book is Beluncle's lack of business ethics. From the beginning Beluncle shows himself devoid of commercial sense, and behind the moral posturing stands a man whose business is sustained by embezzlement and infusions of capital that Beluncle lavishly spends. Here Beluncle's relations with his partner Mrs. Truslove and their associate Mr. Chilly (nearly identical to Mr. Phillimore of "It May Never Happen") afford an excellent opportunity for a thoughtful look at business practices, but Beluncle is too fantastical, too wrapped up in the haze of his own ego and religious delusions to represent anyone beyond himself.

Yet another possibility of this novel is its domestic comedy—the strained and often brutalizing relationships between Beluncle and the other members of his family. He has bullied and humiliated his wife until she has no defense but to become his opposite: "Ethel Beluncle had more courage, but not much more, than her sons. The more Beluncle dressed, the less she dressed: their marriage had always been a duel. . . . The more he sat, the more she stood. The more he was the lord, the more she, vindictively, was the slave" (B, 60). Henry, though he has ambition and a gift for languages, is made to feel guilty about his abilities and humiliated because of his desire to begin a life of his own. George is an emotional spaniel, living to serve his father and receive his approval. Leslie is the healthiest among them, saved by his wit and sense of the absurd, even as he drifts toward easy cynicism and insensitivity. Perhaps it was this side of Beluncle's life that Pritchett intended to emphasize and satirize, but he was unable to sustain the story, subordinate the other elements to it, and give the whole unity and significant form. It is essentially the novel of a short story writer, something Pritchett himself admitted in an interview by saying that *Mr. Beluncle* was written, "when he realized that Maupassant's story of a cad, *Bel Ami,* was in fact a linked series of stories."[5]

In spite of its lack of unity, *Mr. Beluncle* is still an immensely readable and lively comic novel. Elizabeth Bowen's detailed and thoughtful review makes a good case for regarding Beluncle as a major fictional character, saying in part that he is "the indigenous giant of a lower-middle-class jungle of fears and rumours, the manipulator of the success legend, the big boy of the dolls-house suburban and petty business world."[6] She may be right, but there is a hollowness at the center of this complex and inscrutable man that Pritchett either cannot or will not explore. Beluncle fails to arouse sympathy because in the end he is not sufficiently human. He is so wrapped up in self-delusion and solipsism that we draw back from accepting him as representative of ourselves. Nevertheless, *Mr. Beluncle* remains as a monument to Pritchett's final, heroic attempt to conquer the novel form.

Chapter Five
Mature Fiction

Between the appearance of *It May Never Happen* in 1945 and the publication of *When My Girl Comes Home* in 1961, Pritchett concentrated on nonfiction. The interruptions of the war, the stresses of his personal life, and the disappointments of *Mr. Beluncle* conspired to make fiction writing particularly difficult. To these reasons we might add the decline of public interest in the short story and the death of many magazines that traditionally published short fiction. At one point Pritchett abandoned the story altogether. Fortunately, he did not do so permanently, though if he had, his reputation would still be secure, as is evident from the retrospective volume *The Sailor, Sense of Humour, and Other Stories* (1956). This period of relative inactivity gave him time to step back from his art to reconsider his practice and intentions. He had done this briefly in a slender volume called *Why Do I Write?* (1948), consisting of letters on the theory of literature and the place of the writer in society by Pritchett, Elizabeth Bowen, and Graham Greene. Pritchett also contributed a short preface in which he asserted, "If we are asked what, from the social point of view, writers are for, one answer seems to be that they exist to show the inconvenience of human nature; just as from the private point of view, they enlarge human nature's knowledge of itself."[1] Later, discussing the notion that writers must assist in the reformation of society, he says, "The lesson of the thirties seems to be that writers are saved by what can only be called the instinct of party disloyalty" (*W*, 16). These statements summarize his creed and practice, explaining in part why his stories have their peculiar qualities and why, perhaps, they were so coolly received for so long. Reviewing *The Sailor, Sense of Humour, and Other Stories*, Orville Prescott probably spoke for many critics when he said, "Rarely have I read such incontestably good short stories and remained so completely unmoved. It seems a shame to have to say so; but most of these stories are a mite dull."[2] Prescott apparently wants something other than "the inconvenience of human nature"—social relevance or spiritual angst, perhaps. In any event, he represents the admiring indifference with which Pritchett's work has often been greeted. However, the passing of time and the occasion of collecting his best stories for *The Sailor* enabled Pritchett to reflect on his career, and his conclusion, expressed in the preface to the collection, is revealing: "For one, like myself, who has laboriously scattered his time in the writing of novels, literary criticism, and books of travel, the practice of the short story has been the delightful and compensating art and the only kind of writing that has given me great pleasure."[3] How much this realization affected him we cannot tell, but there is a dramatic increase in his production of stories beginning in the mid-fifties. It is as if the voluntary exile had finally returned home.

When My Girl Comes Home and Other Stories

The title story of *When My Girl Comes Home* (1961) is one of Pritchett's longest and most problematic fictions. The technique he uses to present the story is unusual, forcing the reader to follow a tangled series of events narrated out of sequence and involving a large number of characters. In essence we might say that it focuses on the return of Hilda to her mother, old Mrs. Johnson of Hincham Street, London, and on the emotions and conflicts she arouses before leaving again. However, the limited point of view of the narrator, Harry Frazer, forces the reader to deduce events from fragmentary evidence. The story is set shortly after World War II when Britain was beginning to return to normal, although Pritchett does not deal in bombed-out buildings but in bombed-out moral systems. Through Hilda, the residents of Hincham Street are forced to confront the morality of the times, the ethic of survival, beginning with the moment that Hilda steps from the train, sleek and gleaming, to greet everyone with a kiss. For Hincham Street, this is a moment of triumph, the culmination of more than two years of beseeching the bureaucracies of the world for news of their lost daughter, who they thought was a prisoner of the Japanese. Gradually, bits and pieces of a disturbing truth begin to emerge: Hilda did not spend the war as a starved and tortured prisoner but as the wife of a Japanese army officer. Moreover, far from needing the money her mother slaved for by taking in sewing, Hilda has arrived looking prosperous and well-groomed, laden with gifts from two American admirers she met on the way home, one of whom is a writer named Gloster who wants to put her story in a book and on film. The narrator notices that her "face was smooth and blank. . . . I was disturbed by something in her—the lack of history, I think."[4]

While Hilda awaits Mr. Gloster's return, she becomes strangely involved with the neighborhood's genuine prisoner of war, Bill Williams, who learned to survive the death camps: " 'You had to get round the guards,' he said with a wink. 'If you used your loaf a bit, eh? Scrounge around, do a bit of trade' " (38). The women know all too well what sort of trade Hilda has plied, but no one knows what Bill Williams is doing, for he is often seen in unusual places, and his friends smell faintly of the underworld. Sometimes it appears that Williams and Hilda are romantically involved, but when Harry and his fiancée bump into her at a dance, she asks them for protection from Williams, and later that night they discover that Williams has robbed Hilda's flat and disappeared. The following day Hilda vanishes, and the only news that arrives is a photograph of her with her two American boyfriends. Later, when Gloster's book is published, it concerns not Hilda but the people of Hincham Street.

The disjointed narrative technique and the emotional disorder of the characters reflect the confusion Hilda causes and suggest the moral swamp of postwar life. Old values and loyalties have been shattered, held together in the neighborhood only by Mrs. Johnson's faith and vision. When she dies, the new amorality of Hilda and Bill Williams comes into the open; they practice blatantly what others had done secretly, as indicated by the talk in Hincham Street's pub where discussions of the war never proceed very far "because, sooner or later, it came to a closed door in everybody's conscience. There were the men who had shot off trigger fingers, who had got false medical certificates, deserters, ration frauds, black-marketeers, the pilferers of army stores" (42–43). This, then, is a story about "the closed door in everybody's conscience." Pritchett's indirect and perplexing technique was criticized by many reviewers for being overly complex and opaque, but in fact these qualities reflect the theme. The narrator's limited vision mirrors that of the contemporary world in which the facts are seldom clear, and where shifting relationships and ambiguous motives are the new realities. Pritchett shows himself uncannily sensitive to the mood and flavor of the times, and in this story he has found the vehicle for their expression.

Some of the stories in this collection are more traditional in theme and technique. "Just a Little More" is one more look at Walter Pritchett, depicted here as an old man fearing death, talking constantly, and eating voraciously, as if he could by these means keep death at bay. "The Snag" is pure comedy, as sophisticated and glittering as a Restoration play, based on the premise that "The marriages of middle age, the mad impromptus of reason, are the satisfying ones. By that time our obsessions have accumulated and assert their rights, and we find peace in the peculiarities of others" (152). "The Citizen" is a bit too simple, reducing its characters and situations to Freudian case studies. The other stories, however, share with "When My Girl Comes Homes" an awareness of moral and situational complexities and also indicate an expansion of Pritchett's subject matter and range of characters. "On the Scent," for example, confronts us with the perplexing and unusual Manningtree, who at first appears to be an erudite Walter Mitty, lost in a fog of daydreaming about the Inca Indians. He turns out, however, to be a man of prodigious memory and perhaps of remarkable accomplishments as a spy during the war. But we can never be certain of what in his character is genuine. "The Necklace" is a twentieth-century version of Maupassant's famous tale in which a decent, hard-working window washer discovers, when he finds a pearl necklace, that his young wife is an accomplished thief and pathological liar. Pritchett's portrait of this confused and distraught young man is touching and convincing, but his depiction of the half-mad young wife, with her fictitious Aunt Mary and devious manner, is brilliant.

Apart from the title story, however, the most significant is "The Wheelbarrow," in which Pritchett again turns his attention to matters of religion. The story features only two characters, a woman called simply Miss Freshwater's niece and a taxi-driver, handyman, revivalist-preacher named Robert Evans. They meet when she hires his taxi to take her to the house she has inherited and he volunteers to help her clean up when he spies a new green wheelbarrow that for some reason takes his fancy. During the following few days the combination of working closely together and knowing that they will never meet again creates an easy intimacy between them. She teases him about his religion, "deciding what should be 'saved' and what should be 'cast into the flames.' She used those words purposely, as a dig of malice at him" (82). Opening a wardrobe full of dresses, she laments the waste of good material, "Where moth and dust doth corrupt," she misquotes. They work amiably together for two days, destroying decades of family history, until she comes upon mementos of her past that she cannot joke about. Suddenly, dimly remembered images arise from old photographs and her diary, making her feel ill. Remorselessly, Evans forces her to talk about her divorce and the subsequent death of her former husband. She retaliates by asking how he became involved in preaching, and he replies with an "I was the blackest of sinners" conversion story, a mining accident during which he promised God he would reform if he could see his family again. In this respect they are very different, for while thoughts of his family sustained him, hers nearly ruined her. Hearing her tell of parents who could talk only of money and hence drove her into a ruinous marriage, Evans is physically attracted to her, but she is not interested. Squatting by the bonfire, he reminds her of the devil. This exchange weakens the bond between them. A clean break comes when Evans asks what she will do with the wheelbarrow, and she gives it to him. " 'Thank you, ma'am,' he said. It was the first time he had called her 'ma'am.' The word was like a blow. The affair was over. It was, she realized, a dismissal" (98). But she also knows that she no longer needs him and comes to reflect, "He got what he wanted! And I'm evidently not as old as I look" (99).

"The Wheelbarrow" is dramatically constructed, relying almost entirely on dialogue and character interaction for its effects. Pritchett has brought together two type-characters—the gospel preacher and the disillusioned divorcee—and made them into convincing individuals distinguished by background and class but, more important, by speech patterns and gestures. Here, as in many stories, Pritchett's eye for detail and ear for dialogue enable him to lift an apparently trivial episode into a penetrating search for basic values. Evans resembles many of Pritchett's religious characters in being a sensualist beneath the cloth, as indicated by his desire for the wheelbarrow and his advances toward Miss Freshwater's niece. We might dismiss him as a hypocrite if Pritchett did not present him as a man trying in his own way to cope, and in this respect he resembles the woman for whom he briefly works. Both have had to overcome the dark mine of the past, the blackness of guilt and remorse. Evans has found his release in an uneasy bargain with God, while her equivalent of faith comes not from Evan's preaching but from his desire, through which she finds renewed self-esteem. Ironically, Evans may have done his most effective evangelism pursuing a green wheelbarrow.

Key to My Heart

In 1964 *The Key to My Heart* was published as a novel, but in fact it consists of three linked stories that first appeared in the *New Yorker*. Together they make up one of Pritchett's lightest, most engaging, and farcical entertainments, a departure from his usual work in tone and setting. The village atmosphere and broad comedy suggest Fielding or the Larkin novels of H. E. Bates. The stories are narrated by a young man of twenty-four, Bob Fraser, who has recently inherited a bakery and is determined to sort out the shop's tangled finances and collect long-overdue bills from the local gentry. The largest and last debt is owed by Mrs. Brackett, a good-looking woman of forty who uses her position and charms to manipulate everyone, including her husband, a barfly and sports car fancier named Noisy. Their marriage consists mainly of legendary public rows, which generally end with Mrs. Brackett chasing Noisy at high speed through the country lanes until she catches him or runs out of gas. In the process of trying to collect his bills, Bob falls under the spell of Mrs. Brackett's flirtations, becoming so confident that when Noisy asks him for a ride to the station so that he can leave his wife forever, Bob agrees. But the joke is on him. Noisy has left with the money Mrs. Brackett gave him to pay Fraser's bill. In revenge, she writes checks to all the local tradesmen—except Fraser.

In the second story, "Noisy Flushes the Birds," the Bracketts have divorced while Bob Fraser has become engaged to the daughter of a local aristocrat. Neither Bob's mother nor her parents approve. Just as everything appears to be settled, two extraordinary events occur: Mrs. Brackett pays the two hundred pounds she owes Fraser's bakery, and Noisy roars back into town in his Bentley. Mrs. Fraser takes this as a sign that the Bracketts will reconcile, but she is also gruff and nervous, indicating to Bob that something is on her conscience. To celebrate Bob's engagement to Claudia, Mrs. Brackett invites them to dinner, during which Noisy and his friend break in and remove Noisy's valuable collection of stuffed birds. Mrs. Brackett and Bob see them leave and jump in her car to give chase, but, true to form, the car runs out of gas. They spend several hours on a lonely back road, kissing. Claudia cancels the engagement, and Bob is left with the suspicion that somehow his mother engineered everything.

In the third story, "Noisy in the Doghouse," Bob Fraser is no longer the local hero who got Mrs. Brackett to pay her bills but the local fool who lost his fiancée. Rumors are also circulating that Noisy has found a new girl, an Argentine airline stewardess, but when Bob visits, he finds that she is merely a cardboard poster. The next night he calls on Mrs. Brackett for the first time since the fatal dinner party and teases her about Noisy's girlfriend. They end up in bed together. The following day he finds the Argentine stewardess in his garage, put there by Mrs. Brackett, who has burgled Noisy's house. Together Bob and Noisy find her in a country pub. Bob swears his love, but she is furious at having been mocked by the cardboard stewardess and stomps out only to find that Noisy has deflated her tires. She demands that he drive her home and that Bob take care of her car. By the time he pumps air into the tires, the Bracketts have left and are never seen in town again.

Considered as a loosely structured novel, these stories are notable chiefly as entertainment. Especially in the first, the characters are lively and vivid, and the plot is original and provocative. Bob Fraser's youthful confidence makes an excellent contrast to the vanities and wiles of the Bracketts. The duel between Bob and Mrs. Brackett is a humorous, bittersweet mixture of economics and sex, spiced by quarrels between the Bracketts themselves. Noisy at first appears a vapid philanderer with the silly affectation of wearing the key to his heart on a string around his neck, yet he turns out to be more than a match for his wife and her creditor-turned-suitor. Beneath the entertaining, lightly satirical story is a kernel of truth about human nature and the ease with which a Wife of Bath can dupe a young Chanticleer—only to find that a Reynard has fooled them both. The story is technically accomplished, beautifully paced, and engagingly written. In the other two stories focus shifts from character to plot, which is diverting enough to hold our attention but does not take us anywhere significant. It all seems a bit too quaint and remote. The most effective passages are those describing Bob's mother, a fascinating and crotchety widow. Apart from her, there remain only Pritchett's wit and charm, delightful to be sure, entertaining certainly, but in this instance insufficient to provide anything more than a good read.

Blind Love and Other Stories

One of the most remarkable features of Pritchett's career is that he continued to grow and change. A writer in his late sixties might be forgiven for repeating himself or losing the edge of his wit, but Pritchett's style and subject matter remain as fresh and lively in *Blind Love and Other Stories* (1969) as in his earlier collections. If anything, the later stories show a greater variety of characters, settings, and themes than the early ones. Not all the stories in this volume are equally accomplished, but of the ten included, four are of very high quality and two are good, while even the four that fall below par show his characteristic wit and invention.

The minor stories—"The Liars," "The Chain-Smoker," "The Honeymoon," and "Our Oldest Friend"—are typical Pritchett comedies presenting highly individual characters served up in his inimitable style. Entertaining as they are, however, they seem to be character studies for their own sake. If all the stories in this collection resembled these, we might concur with the reviewer who claimed, "what Pritchett seems to be writing is contemporary comedy of humors."[5] Clearly, this is not the case, as can be seen in a more accomplished story, "The Speech," which illustrates the type of problem Pritchett often set for himself. Sally Prosser is the kind of character authors like to satirize and readers find easy to dislike. A seasoned politician, she is addressing a Labour Party rally somewhere in the sleet-lashed north of England, where the audience is small and the evening's arrangements have been poor. As she speaks, she becomes two people: a disembodied voice that skillfully works the crowd without her conscious control, and the person behind the voice, a woman whose mind wanders to her family and the life of commitment she has chosen over domestic comfort. The reader is asked to decide whether she has made the right choice in pursuing social justice at the expense of home and children. Pritchett himself seems ambivalent, sometimes satirizing, sometimes sympathizing. An even more complex character is Phoebe Thwaite of "A Debt of Honor," who feels inferior because she is exceptionally tall and not very attractive. Nine years earlier her husband had fled the country with her money and another woman; now suddenly he is back, asking that she give him £1,200 to repay a gambling debt. By standing up to him, she demonstrates the independence she has earned in the years since he left. Almost perversely, however, she wishes she could have given him the money, for the fact that he returned, swore his love, and made his outrageous request is a compliment that nearly atones for past injuries. This ambivalence gives the story its moment of significant revelation. Phoebe's friends sympathize when they hear her story, "But they saw her eyes shining brilliantly within their gloom."[6]

In the major stories, however, Pritchett's characters come most fully to life. Among these is George Clark of "The Skeleton," eighty-two years old and still vigorous, cantankerous, and aggressive. With his remarkably dark hair and strong constitution he hardly looks his years, though his slight frame, "so paper-thin as to look bodiless" (121), resembles a skeleton. He is also an emotional skeleton, no longer able to love anything, even the art he has so assiduously collected. What he lives for now is victory—over age, his valet, members of his club, and most important, the Great Awful Thing, Death. George's victories begin in the morning, when he rises from his Spartan bed more vigorous than the younger valet who brings his coffee, and continue over lunch at the club where he complains about everything. On this occasion, however, he engages the Arch Enemy, Gaiterswell, who announces that Gloria Archer, the woman George holds responsible for ruining his favorite painter, John Flitestone, will drop in on George with a bundle of Flitestone's letters to sell. A few days later she appears, fiftyish, plump, sleek, drinking George's gin, dredging up old memories, and eventually passing out on his couch. Next morning, George is sick for the first time in his life, and Gloria nurses him. Some weeks later, healthy and back at his club, George once again faces Gaiterswell and tells him that he advised Gloria not to sell the letters. Gaiterswell is surprised, for he understood she needed money. " 'That's not the worst thing to be short of,' sniffed George" (156).

"The Skeleton" is one of Pritchett's outstanding stories. George Clark is a masterful creation. A blend of bitterness, gall, and disappointment, he is both a hateful old crock and a pitiable unfortunate, but this is no sentimental journey into the soft heart of an endearing old codger but an objective, unflinching portrayal of a flawed human being. George's tragedy is not that he has loved and lost, nor that he has never loved at all, but that he has spent most of his life cutting himself off from people in his blind and stupid quest for victory. At the same time, Pritchett shows the fear at the center of George's heart, fear of being turned out of his apartment and of death that stalks him in the east wind. Behind his asceticism and his repeated claims of seeing into the world's frauds and the cheat of organized religion, he feels the moral and emotional emptiness of his life. What rescues the story from pathos is its adroit blend of seriousness and humor. From the beginning George is a comic character fighting for his petty victories, guarding his whiskey from his valet, clinging to his necessary enemies, and disarming his critics by frankly admitting his failings. He is a formidable presence:

> "Oh, God," he groaned loudly, but in a manner so sepulchral and private that people moved respectfully away. It was a groan that seemed to come up from the earth, up from his feet, a groan of loneliness that was raging and frightening to the men around him. (125)

Significantly, the rumbling that formerly symbolized bestial humanity now arouses sympathy. Like the members of George's club, we become genuinely fond of him and, in the end, chuckle that Gloria saves him from himself.

Technically, "The Skeleton" is flawless. In a few pages Pritchett captures the essence of a man and his life by skillfully integrating events from past and present into a composite portrait. Although there are numerous shifts in time, the transitions are flawless. As always, Pritchett's ear for dialogue is acute and his eye for significant detail uncanny: Gloria is a pair of shapely legs, the valet a stoop and a cough, and George is the skeleton, until Gloria puts a bit of meat on his emotional bare bones.

Both "The Cage Birds," with its insightful portrait of two sisters and its complex treatment of materialism, and "The Nest Builder," a delightfully ironic comedy centering on a pair of interior decorators, are well worth attention, but the centerpiece of this volume and one of Pritchett's truly great stories is "Blind Love." This long, complex narrative is a study of two people who feel themselves wounded by God. Mr. Armitage is a lawyer, blind for more than twenty years, while his secretary, Mrs. Johnson, hides a large birthmark extending from her neck almost to her waist. Both have been divorced because of their afflictions, and both suffer emotional crippling along with their physical scars. Armitage has overcome his disability by intelligence and hard work, but this accomplishment has made him proud and insensitive. Mrs. Johnson carries her mark like the stain of sin and lives in a cocoon of self-protection. Both fear humiliation.

The plot traces the relationship between them from the time that Armitage hires Mrs. Johnson until we leave them in Italy, living as man and wife. Crises in their relationship occur because of Armitage's swimming pool. In the first instance, he is enjoying his garden when a dog knocks him off balance and into the pool. Trying to help him change out of his wet clothes, Mrs. Johnson unintentionally humiliates him by deranging his carefully memorized system, thereby reminding him of his dependence on a fixed order. That night, after apologies, they make love for the first time, an act that for her is revenge upon the husband who was revolted by her appearance. She becomes perversely vain of her birthmark, "silently displaying, almost taunting him, when she undressed, with what he could not see" (28). He responds in kind, forcing her on one occasion to rub spittle and dirt on his eyes in a mockery of Christ's miracle.

Shortly after this episode Mrs. Johnson discovers that Armitage has been seeing a faith healer named Smith, yet another version of Walter Pritchett. Smith preaches the unreality of the physical world while being vastly overweight and owning two of everything. Mrs. Johnson begins accompanying Armitage on these visits and in reaction to Smith's talk of divine love confesses for the first time, " 'I love Mr. Armitage as he is' " (48). That evening, shame at having confessed her affection, together with Armitage's questions about whether Smith saw her sunbathing in the nude, produces the climactic confrontation during which she screams:

"I'll tell you something about that Peeping Jesus: he saw the lot. Oh, yes. I hadn't a stitch on. The lot!" she was shouting. And then she started to unzip her dress and pull it down over her shoulder and drag her arm out of it. "You can't see it, you silly fool. The whole bloody Hebrides, the whole plate of liver." (50)

Moments later the cook finds her face down in the pool, though how she got there we are not told. In his panic to help Armitage forgets everything he knows about the house and gropes helplessly while others rescue her. This second accident erases their differences by equalizing them in a kind of secular baptism and forcing them to confront their interdependence. From this time on they live in Italy, where he depends entirely on her and they enjoy not a perfect love but an understanding one.

"Blind Love" is among Pritchett's most powerful stories, a painfully honest depiction of two wounded people salvaging dignity in spite of their failings and limitations. Their handicaps, however, are less important in themselves than as metaphors for human limitations and the ways by which people exploit their wounds as weapons. Significantly, Mr. Armitage and Mrs. Johnson emerge as less handicapped than the ostensibly whole Mr. and Mrs. Smith, whose marriage is built not on shared needs or affection but on habit and subjugation. Unifying the story beyond the theme of wholeness and handicap is its religious imagery, particularly the suggestions of baptism brought about through the accidents in the swimming pool. These wash the central figures of their pride and pretensions and unite them in a common humanity that they have tried to deny by hiding behind veneers of confidence and indifference. Wet and vulnerable, they grow in mutual understanding and self-knowledge. Thus, the story suggests, without sentimentality or special pleading, that while love may be blind, it is not unseeing. Above all, perhaps, it is accepting.

The Camberwell Beauty and Other Stories

The Camberwell Beauty and Other Stories (1975) is a remarkable collection in a number of ways, not least because it comes from the pen of a man now well past retirement age. Of course, the basic methods and concerns have not changed: he still writes about the quirks and frustrations of the middle class, but some of his characters in this collection are surprisingly young. "The Rescue" is an amusing tale narrated by a liberated sixteen-year-old girl who seduces a reluctant young librarian in the park, but far more authentic is an obviously autobiographical story, "The Diver," set in the Paris of Pritchett's youth. Here we have for the final time the would-be author and puritan, proud of his virginity even though he suffers the teasing of his fellow workers and the scorn of Mme Chamson, a provocative woman of forty who runs a dry-cleaning service. When a bargeload of leather goods is sunk in the Seine, the narrator and his friend are sent to oversee salvaging operations and spend a delightful week watching a diver rescue the sodden bales. On the last day the young man is accidentally knocked into the river. Mme Chamson comes along shortly afterward and takes him to her shop for a change of clothes. Ordered to undress, the boy is embarrassed to find that he has an erection. Mme Chamson becomes angry at his impudence and stalks out of the room, leaving him half-dressed and unable to move. After a few minutes she calls to him, and he finds her lying nude on the bed. He has never seen a naked woman before, but when she taunts him with his inexperience, he improvises a lurid tale about finding a murdered woman naked in her bed when he was twelve. Mme Chamson is touched by his fiction. " 'Ah,' she laughed, pulling at my trousers. 'The diver's come up again. Forget, Forget.' "[7] This encounter not only makes the young man the office hero instead of its goat, but it also changes him profoundly. Before making love to Mme Chamson, he had been trying to write fiction but could not find the words. Manufacturing a lie to cover his innocence releases his creative powers. Through this comedy Pritchett has found new expression for an old theme, the connection between sexuality and creativity, a connection that is both generally true and, as we have seen, has particular relevance to Pritchett's own experience. Beyond this, "The Diver" is a classic tale of innocence and experience, refreshingly humorous without losing seriousness.

"The Marvellous Girl" represents another innovation in Pritchett's short fiction, depending for its effects less on character than on depicting the pressure of intensely dramatic moments. The narrative line consists of episodes linked in associative rather than chronological order from which we construct the story of an artist named Francis, two years divorced: "The marriage was one of those prickly friendships that never succeeded—to *his* astonishment, at any rate—in turning into love, but are kept going by curiosity" (46). Events preceding and during a banquet attended by the narrator, his ex-wife, and a secretary he calls simply "the marvellous girl" make up the story. The most important of these is the moment immediately after the lights fail when Francis almost panics because he fears he will not be able to find the girl. As he gropes his way toward her, the pressure of the crowd, the confusion of darkness, and the unspoken tension between Francis and his ex-wife, sharing the same occasion but no longer the same life, are evoked with vivid immediacy. For eight pages we are caught up in the young man's struggle to reach the girl, while simultaneously bits of previous conversations, quarrels with his ex-wife, and recollected meetings with the girl reveal why the marriage broke up and how he came to know the moment before the lights failed that he must find "the marvellous girl." Somehow, she finds him. There follows a scene of almost unbearable tension in which Francis and the girl stand together holding hands while the crowd passes by, including his ex-wife and her new lover. For an instant, the buttons of her coat catch on his: "it seemed to him as long as their marriage" (57). The momentary union of the buttons is a brilliant symbol of their relationship, superficial and brief, a matter of friction rather than love. When the buttons release, the divorce becomes emotionally valid. Francis and the girl go out a back door, searching for the darkness where lovers hide.

It is easy to miss or minimize the technical perfection of this story. The narrative elements have to be fitted together like pieces in an elaborate puzzle without interfering with the emotional shades and nuances to create a moment at which one relationship ends and another is born. Both purposes must be satisfied without elaborate exposition. Beyond the technical perfection of the story are the human and thematic elements that make us care about these characters. This is a short story for connoisseurs.

The centerpiece of the collection, however, is the long title story that might serve as an example of quintessential Pritchett. Complex in structure and oblique in movement, it takes us into the subculture of London's antique dealers, where each man's "mind is on his specialty, and within that specialty there is one object he broods on from one year to the next, most of his life: the thing a man would commit murder to get his hands on if he had the nerve. . ." (3). The narrator, a former antique dealer, focuses on two collectors: August, who specializes in ivories, and Pliny, an elderly bachelor. The link among these three men is August's niece, who grows up to be a beauty and the unlikely wife of Pliny. The narrator's goal is to seduce her away from her elderly husband, who treats her less as a wife than as an objet d'art. During the day he makes her dress in a soldier's costume and bang on a drum to frighten burglars away, and his nighttime habits are no less strange:

> "He is not a real husband, a real lover," I said.
> "Yes, he is," she said proudly. "He takes my clothes off before I go to bed. He likes to look at me. I am the most precious thing he has."
> "That isn't love, Isabel," I said.
> "It is," she said with warmth. (38)

Remarkably, Pritchett makes us believe that the bizarre events of this story are real, largely by the air of authority in the narrator. He has the surface details of this strange culture so convincingly right that we do not question the probability of Pliny's lovemaking or of the other strange events. This is reinforced by the symbolic validity of the situation, love as pride of ownership. The girl is reduced to her commercial value. She is literally a sex object, but whether the narrator's interest in her is any less possessive remains open to speculation. The theme of love as possession relates to the narrator's observation that antique dealers feed on illusion. After a final attempt to seduce Isabel the narrator walks out into the London night and observes, "How unreal people looked in the sodium light" (41). Like some of Pritchett's other stories, this one presents a strange subculture that is both real in itself and representative of society at large.

The other stories in the collection do not attain the heights of these three, but all have their points of interest. "Our Wife" presents an unusual lovers' triangle featuring a woman whose appetite for talk is so strong that she needs two men in her life at all times. "The Spree" is a warmly comic depiction of Walter Pritchett in his last years, accidentally finding himself on a company outing he has no business attending. It contains Pritchett's most sympathetic portrait of his father. "The Last Throw" is another story in the series about the film world, in which both the film magnate Karvo and his clever assistant Chatty are outwitted by a scheming woman. "The Lady from Guatemala" exposes the hypocrisy of a left-wing newspaper editor, while "Did You Invite Me?" is yet another complex comedy of middle-aged love and its rocky road to marriage. As one reviewer remarked in commenting on this collection, *"The Camberwell Beauty* provides, above all, a gaggle of characters, solid, particular, and knowable."[8]

On the Edge of the Cliff

By the late 1970s Pritchett was finally gaining the recognition he had so long deserved. Perhaps the knighthood in 1975 was the catalyst, or his two volumes of autobiography, or the superb biographies of Balzac and Turgenev. Whatever the reason, Pritchett's genius for the short story was acknowledged in a variety of ways and by a number of perceptive critics, not least among them Eudora Welty, an outstanding short story writer herself. Reviewing the 1978 retrospective collection *Selected Stories,* Miss Welty enthusiastically remarked on Pritchett's unique powers:

any Pritchett story is all of it alight and busy at once, like a well-going fire. Wasteless and at the same time well fed, it shoots up in flame from its own spark like a poem or a magic trick, self-consuming, with nothing left over. He is one of the great pleasure-givers in our language.[9]

A year later Benjamin DeMott echoed these observations in a stimulating review of Pritchett's last volume of new stories, *On The Edge of the Cliff* (1979):

The wit, pungency and spirit familiar from the past remain unchanged. But together with the psychological penetration there's a calm, surely-judged understanding of how we would like human relations to go, and of what, if we could have our way, we'd want to be able to expect of ourselves in our dealings with others. In a word, the nature of V. S. Pritchett's gift is coming clearer as, in high health and vitality, with 30 volumes behind him and creative powers sustained, he enters his 80th year. It appears that moral intelligence lies as close as anything to its core.[10]

The moral intelligence had been there all along, but what many readers found astonishing was that Pritchett continued to apply it to such a wide variety of characters and experiences.

Three of the stories in this collection, "The Vice-Consul," "The Worshippers," and "The Spanish Bed," concern one of Pritchett's recurring themes, the ways by which people build realities for themselves and the difficulties they face when these constructions encounter something unassimilable. A comic version of this idea occurs in "The Vice-Consul," in which a no-nonsense official finds himself dealing with a fantastic product of the tropics, a sailor named McDowell who comes to him for advice on how to retrieve his false teeth from a young woman he "accidentally" slept with. McDowell's incredible yarn illustrates not so much the simple lie as the need for self-deception, the universal propensity to prefer a face-saving delusion to the truth. The best of these three stories is "The Spanish Bed," for retired mining engineer Dr. Billeter is a representative of the contemporary passion for "facts." In pursuing information about the life of his favorite author, Billeter meets a woman whose subjective vision momentarily unsettles his comfortable assumptions about objective reality. Watching these two worldviews collide provides both lively entertainment and a dramatic rendering of a complex idea. "Tea With Mrs. Bittell" touches on the theme of self-delusion but concentrates on the problems of communication between classes and generations. Once again the protagonist is difficult to judge, for she is both a lonely, sympathetic figure and a disagreeable snob.

The remaining stories touch on some aspect of love, three on infidelity. In "A Family Man" an outraged wife confronts her husband's mistress, who skillfully lies her way out of difficulty. In the process, however, she discovers that her lover is also betraying her with yet a third woman. "The Fig Tree" is far more subtle and complex in dealing with the theme of the betrayer betrayed. Pritchett traces a love triangle through its complex emotions and deceptions until it comes full circle, with the husband ending up in the role of lover and the lover dwindling into domesticated boredom. However, the best of the love triangle stories is "The Accompanist." Here, as in "The Fig Tree," we can detect the influence of Henry James on Pritchett's psychological and narrative techniques. The lovers' triangle consists of the narrator William, his mistress Joyce, and her impotent husband Bertie. Joyce is an accompanist by profession and also in personality. William observes, "She sang and played as if she did not exist,"[11] and elsewhere notes that she always appears to be awaiting a voice or tune dictated by another. Bertie needs her support, for he is an orphan, raised by a public school headmaster. His only family link is a collection of preposterously ugly Victorian furniture inherited from an aunt. Thus he is less an individual than part of a group, and his friends "were a kind of society for cosseting him" (118). His decaying Victorian flat and ugly furniture suggest decadent exhaustion, an attitude he flaunts by singing a French music-hall song about a bride murdered on her wedding night. It is an ironic song for Bertie and Joyce, for whom "wedding nights were an academic subject." William narrates the story as if privy to everyone's secrets, recording changes in mood and perception with Jamesian sensitivity. Communication among Bertie's friends occurs by vibrations and telepathy, and William's passion to know secrets is reflected in his repeated use of bone imagery. At one point he envisions Joyce bathing naked in a cold stream, "all bones," and at another point he thinks of her as having "the look of a girl who has a strange shame of her bones" (119). Thus, the revelation that comes to him during the bawdy song is especially crushing, for he realizes, "I lived by my desire; *they* had the intimacy of eating" (122). He, too, is an accompanist, through whom readers are given a penetrating glance into the psychology of love and at the barriers that separate individuals, even lovers.

The title story of the collection, "On the Edge of the Cliff," deals with an old literary theme, the December-May relationship. Harry is a retired botanist in his seventies, while Rowena is an artist in her mid-twenties. Others marvel at their affair, but to Harry and Rowena

"There are rules for old men who are in love with young girls, all the stricter when the young girls are in love with them. It has to be played as a game" (3). Thus, both pretend on occasion to be jealous, and both avoid anything that emphasizes the difference in their ages. At a local fair Harry meets a former mistress, Daisy Pyke, and a young man named Stephen he assumes is her son. Unnerved by this fragment of the past, Harry takes Rowena for a walk along the seaside cliffs to Withy Hole, a deep cave that has always fascinated him because of its infinite spaces and threat of danger. To Rowena it is a "meaningless wound. . . . It reminded her of his mouth when she had once seen it (with a horror she tried to wipe from her mind) before he had put his dentures in" (11). Defying age, the elements, and his own rule, Harry strips and dives into the frigid water. "He had dived in boastfully and in a kind of rage, a rage against time, a rage against Daisy Pyke too" (13).

A few days later, Daisy calls on Harry while Rowena is shopping. He fears an ulterior motive, but she has only a simple request: that he keep Rowena away from her lover, Stephen. When Rowena learns that Stephen is not Daisy's son, she is shocked:

"You can't mean that," she said, putting on a very proper air. "She's old enough—" but she stopped, and instead of giving him one of her light hugs, she rumpled his hair. "People do confide in you, I must say," she said. I don't think I like her coming up here. Tell me what she said." (20)

Thus the story ends, and we can be certain that Harry will not tell her what Daisy said.

Part of Pritchett's purpose in this story is to challenge conventional notions about relationships between old and young, but more important is the depiction of Harry, Daisy, and Rowena as people. Daisy, and to a greater extent Harry, are literally walking the edge of the cliff; age and the risks they take with young lovers make their lives precarious. We are perhaps shocked by these pairs of lovers, but to Pritchett such affairs are vital signs of defiance, like Harry's foolhardy dive into the cold Atlantic. Old age is not a time to wait passively for death. It is as much a part of life as youth. It does change the rules of love, but it does not create barriers so much as intensify those that always exist. The games Harry plays with Rowena are no more necessary than those played by couples of any age. Limitations must be overlooked, differences accommodated. Love must be treated as a fragile relationship needing such stimulants as deliberate jealousy and departure from habit. All ages walk the edge of the cliff.

Technically as well as thematically this is an exciting and disturbing story. Pritchett's sense of form is faultless as he combines the trivial details of ordinary life into a significant pattern. The opening sentences, for example, rivet our attention and set precisely the right mood:

The sea fog began to lift towards noon. It had been blowing in, thin and loose for two days, smudging the tops of the trees up the ravine where the house stood. "Like the cold breath of old men," Rowena wrote in an attempt at a poem, but changed the line, out of kindness, to "the breath of ghosts," because Harry might take it personally. (3)

Throughout, the prose retains this lean yet suggestive simplicity, and as always there are those unexpected turns of phrase and flashes of insight that make any Pritchett story a pleasure to read: "But there it is—one must expect it when one is old: the map in one's head, indeed the literal map of the country empties and loses its contours, towns and villages, and people sink out of sight. The protective faces of friends vanish and one is suddenly alone, naked and exposed" (7). The symbolism is equally bold yet unobtrusive, as in the sea-washed cave that evokes both the pleasures of the past and the fear of death. "On the Edge of the Cliff" demonstrates Pritchett's continuing vitality and his rightful claim to the title as "the best living short story writer."[12]

Chapter Six
Nonfiction

Travel Writing

Since he left London at age twenty, Pritchett's passions have been writing and travel, which he has often combined in books and articles about most of the major countries and regions of the world, except the Far East. The English tradition of travel writing is long and honorable, stretching back at least as far as Sir John Mandeville's *Travels* in the fourteenth century and receiving a powerful boost in the nineteenth century from a long list of important writers, male and female, including Dickens, Mrs. Trollope, and Harriet Martineau. Pritchett's immediate models were Hilaire Belloc and D. H. Lawrence, but he has since become very much his own man, applying to travel writing the same interest in character and scenic details that he shows in his fiction.

The Spanish Temper (1954) is the best of Pritchett's travel books. A lifetime's observations, analysis, and reading are condensed into a modest-sized book, nearly every page of which contains persuasive and illuminating remarks. In structure *The Spanish Temper* resembles *Marching Spain.* This time the route begins in France and takes him through the Pyrenees and Basque country, southwest to Miranda, Madrid, Andalusia, Seville, Granada, and Murcia on the Mediterranean, thence northward to Valencia, Tarragona, and finally to Barcelona. He makes no attempt to be comprehensive or to visit the conventional tourist sites of each region, although he does take us to the Escorial, the Prado, and the bullring in Seville. Pritchett's observations are not intended for the casual tourist, for the book "assumes the reader has at any rate read his Guide."[1] His purpose is not to direct the traveler to the picturesque but to discuss the Spanish character in all its richness, idiosyncrasy, and variety. He is the novelist as traveler and observer, creating a composite character from many individuals, balancing the particular and the general. With few exceptions, he focuses less on monuments and landscape than on people, assuming that his readers are at least generally familiar with Spain's history, government, politics, and travel-poster stereotypes. Nor is the book a showcase for its author's cleverness or personality, though the man who writes comes through as observant, witty, ironic, fair-minded, and cosmopolitan.

The first chapter illustrates Pritchett's method and provides a summary of many of his main points. In an amusing description of two Spaniards he depicts people who talk endlessly around the topic with a self-absorption and indirection that produce conversation like "knitting, so fine is the detail, so repetitious the method" (9). They are fiercely proud and individual, almost solipsistic; suspicious of foreigners yet friendly to travelers; regionalists first, Spaniards incidentally; contemptuous of the supposed benefits of industrialism, yet wrapped in a bureaucracy so stifling that Pritchett can compare it only with that of nineteenth-century Russia. Spain's harsh geography and climate have produced a people of extremes, among whom the virtues of tolerance and open-mindedness are in little evidence, for the Spanish see everything as black or white.

One theme to which Pritchett returns frequently is the Spanish sense of personal pride and dignity. In spite of their fanaticism and their insistence on doctrinal purity, the Spanish have fashioned a fierce individualism and profound sense of self. In part, he argues, their dignity derives from a deep conservatism regarding custom and from their rejection of industrialism, which has enabled them to preserve personality. Mass man does not exist in Spain because the tools for creating him have been rejected. Insisting on the dignity of the individual leads to an egalitarianism found nowhere else in Europe: "The Spanish live in castes, but not in classes, and their equality—the only real equality I have met anywhere in the world—is in their sense of nobility or, rather, in the sense of the absolute quality of the person" (45). Not surprisingly, these attributes are reflected in personal bearing and dress, which are not like the European and American mania for fashion: "Any Spanish crowd, even in the poor districts, is the best-dressed crowd in Europe, but they are rarely elegant or fashionable. They have simply a firm conservative sense of what is fitting, not of what attracts extravagant attention" (84). Custom, dress, and dignity of bearing come together in the nightly *paseo,* the procession about the town or city square, when cafés are crowded and Spain carries on her public social life. Pritchett finds the Spaniards an attractive people: "The Spaniard level [of looks] is high; indeed a certain regularity of feature, boldness of nose, and brilliance of eye appear to have been standardized. . . . One has the impression of great natural vitality, undistracted by northern nerves" (85–86). Attractive as their individualism is, it leads to an almost comic absorption in the self, the egoism Pritchett described in the Spaniards talking on the station platform. The Spaniard has difficulty recognizing anyone beyond himself. In art, this creates an intensely individual quality in the masters but also an impoverished imagination, "for their powerful egotism has been of the kind that cannot put itself in another creature's place or transcend its own personality" (119).

To most Westerners a strong sense of individual worth would suggest liberalism in thought and politics, but this is the country of the Inquisition, Loyola's Jesuits, and General Franco. Pritchett deals unapologetically with this paradox and traces it to another contradiction, the Spanish love of anarchy. He sees Spain's history as dominated by civil war, in particular the six centuries of struggle to oust the Moors:

> The Spanish effort to impose the Catholicism of the Counter-Reformation, to be the apostles and soldiers of the only truly reformed Catholic faith, to rule in that name, and to prevent by exhaustive means every deviation was a continuation in Europe of over six hundred years of war against the Moorish occupation. (53)

In postwar Spain this spirit is the soul of Franco's dictatorship, toward which Pritchett is surprisingly lenient. In the Spain of mid-twentieth-century political discussion was forbidden, though Spaniards continued to argue politics openly and passionately, but in Pritchett's view the country was too exhausted by civil war to oppose Franco actively or even to complain very much about his rule. Pritchett's anti-establishment feelings are directed against ecclesiastical rather than civil authorities:

> The authority of the Church in Spain has passed out of the spiritual life into the social, political, and temporal. There one meets the packed committee, the Party nominees, the infiltrations of the members of Opus Dei who work, exactly in Communist fashion, to frustrate professional groups. It is impossible for a foreigner to state or judge the extent of the struggle: the liberty of the press has gone, and it is as impossible to publish an anti-clerical view, or one hostile to the view of the Church on any matter in Spain, as it would be to advocate private capitalism or non-official views in Russia. (118–19)

Overall, however, Pritchett accepts the totalitarian strain in the Spanish temper without judgment, and the book is the better for this. When he does discuss politics, as in a long passage in chapter 4, he is dull.

He is equally tolerant of Spain's lack of "modern" facilities and its alleged "inefficiency." Even in the mid-1950s Spain seemed almost medieval in pace and Victorian in technology. Much work was still done by animals; roads were poor and cars were few, Spain being the only major European country at the time not to have an automobile industry. Trains were slow, the stations in bad repair, and employees dawdled over their work, but the apparent indolence and inefficiency are not what they seem. Pritchett perceives a national passion for "facilitating" matters. Spaniards despise official channels because these do not work. A friend, a relative, the hanger-on of a hanger-on will use "influence" to register a car, secure a permit, or seal a contract. It is the inevitable system in a poor country, where every job attracts a collection of dependents and ostensible assistants. In Pritchett's view inefficiency was an admirable form of rebellion and another facet of the Spanish temper—a genius for drawing blueprints but a reluctance to build anything. In the Spanish proverb "We obey but we do not fulfill," which he quotes several times, lies part of the explanation. Indeed, according to Pritchett, fascism was losing its grip on Spain because the Spanish were "indolently nullifying it" (209).

No discussion of the Spanish character can avoid the bullring, and here again Pritchett is neither apologist nor detractor. To him bullfighting is a fact, something to be observed and understood. These are people of strong feeling, whose religion is soaked in the blood of Christ and the martyrs, who are not squeamish and who can be cruel. Death holds special fascination for the Spanish. Pritchett traces the bullfight to its Moorish origins, through its period as an aristocratic sport, to its present position as popular spectacle. To Pritchett, it is now "a play in three acts" (188) whose outcome is predictable, but of course it is not the result that people pay to watch but the art of fighting the bull. Pritchett maintains, "Bullfighting is not a sport, and it is therefore not a cruel sport. It is a ritual and a ceremony" (178). He refuses to pass moral judgment on a custom he only partially understands, but he does find it ultimately boring because of its ritual: "it is one more example of the peculiar addiction to the repetitive and monotonous in the Spanish nature" (180).

Reviewers commenting on *The Spanish Temper* were almost unanimously laudatory, praising the book for accomplishing its intention of dissecting and communicating the Spanish psyche. In this regard it remains valuable and perceptive, even though Franco is no longer in power and Spain is fast becoming a fully European country, complete with heavy industry and a rapid rate of urbanization. Madrid, for example, which seemed to Pritchett an artificial capital, is assuming its place as a cosmopolitan city and the center of Spanish life and culture. Nevertheless, it will be a long time before Pritchett's book goes out of date, and as travel literature it is destined for an honorable place. As one reviewer aptly said, "He sees the country for what it is, magnificent, indeed, but also harsh, morbid, excessive and obtuse; and he never for a moment abandons his own point of view, remaining throughout ironic, humane, dispassionate and English to the core."[2]

London, New York, Dublin

In collaboration with German photographer Evelyn Hofer, Pritchett published three large "coffee table" books: *London Perceived* (1962), *New York Proclaimed* (1965), and *Dublin: A Portrait* (1967). Although the books are fully illustrated with Hofer's photographs, Pritchett's text is not merely an extended caption or superfluous accompaniment. In all three, text and pictures work together to provide a coherent view of the city.

Of the three, *London Perceived* is by far the best. Having spent a lifetime anatomizing individual Londoners, Pritchett is uniquely qualified to comment on them in general. Characteristically, he sees them as essentially middle-class, intensely respectable, and divided into endless little clubs, coteries, neighborhoods, and clans. Londoners, he claims, love to join groups, however eccentric, and this is reflected in the organization of the city, which is not a genuine metropolis but a collection of villages. These in turn are subdivided into innumerable squares, closes, terraces, and cul-de-sacs. Consequently, while London is an international city with countless commercial, political, and personal ties to the rest of the world, it is unlike any other European capital in having no central place where residents meet. Except in moments of national celebration, Londoners do not gather at Trafalgar Square or Piccadilly Circus but remain attached to their neighborhoods. From this habit of mind and character springs some of the Londoner's freedom and sense of privacy. These

are middle-class virtues, and it is the middle class Pritchett cele-
brates. He takes us only occasionally into noble houses of the aristoc-
racy and even less often into the slums of the poor. He is far more at
home in churches, markets, small gardens, public parks, antique
shops, riverboats, and pubs where ordinary people work, play, and
congregate. Hofer's photographs take the same approach, preferring
small and anonymous places, interesting details, and the faces of London's people to grand vistas or panoramas. One fancies on occasion
that one of Pritchett's fictional characters has agreed to pose for
Hofer's camera. Similarly, it is as a commercial and trading center
that Pritchett discusses London's history and development. He particularly notes the many anachronistic offices, rights, customs, and tra-
ditions originating from ancient assertions of rights connected to
something monetary or commercial. For Pritchett, modern London
begins not with the flamboyant and expansive Elizabethans but with
the dour and industrious puritans.

Characteristic, too, is the way Pritchett traces the history of London through the individuals who built and lived in it. He lays far
more stress on Pepys, Evelyn, Wren, Inigo Jones, Hogarth, and even
Nicholas Barebones (speculative builder and son of the infamous
"Praise-God" Barebones) than he does on any monarch. Pritchett's
London is the moiling, toiling marketplace of Daniel Defoe and the
grimy theater of Dickens, not the home of parliaments and empire
builders. Even more important than the individual stamp of famous
architects is the collective impress of anonymous builders. "This London has often been denounced as a monotonous collection of little
boxes; it seemed 'soulless' to some Victorians. For myself, the London
of the little houses, whether they are in Harley Street or Chelsea, Is-
lington or Kensington, and the millions of little chimneys, is the true
London."[3] Not surprisingly, his spokesman for Victorian London is
Dickens, and he finds the contemporary city full of Dickensian characters. The twentieth century belongs to mass man, the mobs who
plod through Westminster Abbey, flock to London's pageants, and
immigrate from all over the world to make it a truly cosmopolitan
city.

London Perceived is written affectionately from the inside and neither
glorifies nor denigrates its subject. One detects in the style an extra
measure of spice and enthusiasm. Often the prose tumbles along in well-
controlled vigor, with almost Victorian fullness and ornamentation:

After the fixation on property, privacy, and order; after the preference for the arguments of the parliamentary to the happiness of the democratic; after our conviction that some of the inalienable right to life, liberty, and the pursuit of happiness had better be looked at twice at least; after the guilty feeling that to sit down and just watch the crowd go by for an hour or so for the price of a beer or a cup of tea is idle, bad for trade, and that in any case it is rude to stare—would you like people to stare at you?—after all these things, there is the unanswerable climate. (16)

The great charm of the book is its focus on London's people and its intimate appraisal of London's character and soul. The writing is lucid, lively, and colorful; the observations are balanced and insightful; the impressions are immediate and sensual. As much as Pritchett's fiction, this is a lyric tribute to the energy, good humor, and even snobbery of the British middle classes in all their brick-and-mortar ordinariness.

New York Proclaimed is similar in organization and format to *London Perceived,* yet in spite of many lively and perceptive passages it is less successful. As many British travel writers have shown, the outsider's eye often notices what the insider misses, but the great virtue of *London Perceived* is its intimate knowledge of the subject, something the New York book lacks. Pritchett is astute about the physical appearance of New York, as when he describes the road from any American airport to the city as the "the modern nightmare. It has been designed to shock the sky visitor with the full visual horror of the life of industrial man fighting for his place in the dormitory, choked by products."[4] In most other respects the book is not outstanding. Perhaps the most original and illuminating passages are those that trace the growth of the city from its rude beginnings as a Dutch colony through its chaotic cycles of growth and decay to its present eminence. Pritchett has a genius for summary and distillation, for capsule biography and the thumbnail sketch. This portion of the book also shows an impressive variety of literary and historical allusion, deriving from a long acquaintance with American literature and culture. It would be difficult to find a more lively, readable, and perceptive analysis of New York's history in so brief an account. Outside this chapter, however, the illuminating passages are few, although occasionally one finds a gem:

But when one hears a New Yorker say he has no time to think or feel or

be, one must understand that the drilling, the "constant flicker" of the ma-
chine, delights him more, whatever he may say to the contrary. . . . The
high regard for psychiatry indicates that the psyche, the soul, the affective
areas of our nature are thought of in terms of adjustable mechanisms. The
wheels of our psyche should run smoothly: the New Yorker spends a lot of
time inspecting them. (65)

These, however, prove to be rare moments. Most of the text is
solid, interesting, well written, and lively, but uninspired. The wide
variety of New York's people is unrepresented; the extremes of its
wealth and poverty, violence and indolence, artistry and vulgarity are
mentioned but not deeply felt or expressed. There is a tendency
toward cliché—the pace of life, the rudeness of bus drivers, the gar-
rulity of taxi drivers, the angularity of the city's streets and architecture. The chapter on Greenwich Village is without distinction, and
the attempts at sociological analysis in the chapter on Harlem lack
conviction. To say that *New York Proclaimed* is not up to Pritchett's
usual standard, however, is not to condemn it so much as to emphasize the expectations we have of anything he writes.

Dublin: A Portrait is similar in all essentials to the previous two
volumes, but in being once again an intimate study by one who
knows the city well, it resembles the London volume more. Pritchett
is not Irish, but he is more at home in Dublin than New York. His
thesis is that Dublin copes with a unique set of tensions and contradictions that make it unlike any other European capital. He stresses
in part its non-European character because of its position as the west-
ernmost outpost of Europe and its being a seaport, which automati-
cally makes the city a frontier. Thus, Dubliners resemble the
Russians and the Spanish, who are also marginally European, and the
Jews, who have long been a race but seldom a nation. Another stress
in Dublin's life derives from the natural liberalism of its status as a
port versus the deeply ingrained conservatism of its often fanatical Ca-
tholicism. These are in addition to the deep religious and political
divisions in Ireland that have led paradoxically to a taste for heroes
and tragedy as well as a penchant for "the great evasion of the
laugh."[5] So fundamental are the dualities that "the double face, one
containing the outer, the other the inner life, is very general. . ." (29).

Pritchett begins his study with personal recollections dating from
1923, when he was sent as a young reporter to cover the turmoil resulting from the Easter Uprising of 1916. In the last chapter he re-

turns to this central event in modern Irish history by visiting Kilmainham Jail, a notorious British prison then being converted to a tourist attraction. Between these chapters he examines Dublin's people, theater, writers, architecture, and above all the colorful figures in government, politics, and the arts who have shaped the city over the centuries. Georgian and early Victorian Dublin most delight the modern eye, though many of the finest buildings are lamentably in danger of destruction. The spacious streets and gardens are, he finds, the only positive achievements of absentee landlords and British governors, the relative cleanliness of the city the sole positive result of its chronic lack of industry. Tracing Dublin's history from the Norman invasions to the Easter Uprising, Pritchett moves with confidence through a bewildering array of conquerors, patriots, villains, scoundrels, heroes, and eccentrics. Along the way he makes frequent and witty comparisons with present attitudes and ideas, thus making history a living part of the city. For the inexpert there is too much to digest and too little explanation, but to those familiar with Ireland Pritchett's genius for distillation and summary is obvious. Occasionally, the prose bogs down under the weight of anecdote, but most of the time it slides along smoothly, a happy combination of general observation, minute detail, and vivid description and narration:

> If the hero of [the early nineteenth century] was Wolfe Tone, the villain of the Union was Edward Fitzgibbon, Earl of Clare who was determined to dish Pitt's policy of Catholic emancipation. The Dublin mob hated him. A few years before he had obtained the withdrawal of Lord Fitzwilliam, a popular, liberal viceroy; the Dublin crowd rioted and went to Fitzgibbon's house in Ely Place, with a rope to hang him. Two good things can be said for Fitzgibbon: Dublin owed the Wide Road Commission to him and the Customs House.
>
> When he died, the mob pelted his coffin with dead cats. (64)

Pritchett must certainly be reckoned among the finest travel writers of his day, not only for the books discussed here, but equally for the many magazine essays he has published over the years, a number of which were collected in *The Offensive Traveller* (1964; English title *Foreign Faces*). The title derives from Pritchett's observation that "I travel, therefore I offend. I represent that ancient enemy of all communities: the stranger."[6] Perhaps so, but if all travelers were as tolerant as he and wrote as engagingly and perceptively about their experiences, few would complain.

The Critical Essays

Pritchett's career as a critic began in 1926 when his reviews first appeared in various London periodicals. From that time a steady stream of literary articles and reviews has poured from his pen, so many that a complete bibliography would run to many pages. Most of these were produced for the *New Statesman,* from which were taken most of the essays that comprise his collections *In My Good Books* (1942), *The Living Novel* (1946, reissued as *The Living Novel and Later Appreciations,* 1964), *Books in General* (1953), *The Working Novelist* (1965), *The Myth Makers* (1979), *The Tale Bearers* (1980), and *A Man of Letters* (1985).

Most commentators on Pritchett's criticism note that he continues the nineteenth-century tradition of the essayist and man of letters and is in this respect out of step with the twentieth-century critics who rely on ideology and methodology. Although he fits loosely into the liberal camp, he belongs to no school of criticism, espouses no particular methodology, and speaks for no party or clique. He is an individualist, speaking in his own voice, making his own judgments, and standing on his own authority. In so doing he takes a middle path, avoiding on the one hand the slickness of hip journalists and on the other the ponderous solemnities of academicians. To some extent his approach has been dictated by the space limitations and audience of the *New Statesman* "where the writer has to get at an essence, show his wit and his hand, and make his decisive effect with alacrity in fewer than 2000 scrupulous words. . . ."[7] Still, Pritchett's criticism, like his fiction, is shaped less by external factors than by the idiosyncrasies of his intellect and temperament, which have always set him apart from the mainstream and given his works their individual stamp. Even if he were less perceptive, his individuality would be sufficient to make his essays lively and interesting.

For all his independence of judgment, Pritchett is no mere impressionist. There is a solid theoretical foundation beneath his maverick attitude, but he does not make a fetish of methodology or allow a priori assumptions to dictate literary judgments. His method is to approach each author and work on its own terms, to search out excellences and lapses as they appear within the aesthetic suggested by the work itself. This is an approach depending not on ideology but on perception, sympathy, and eclectic taste. It also puts a premium on sensitivity and a willingness to take risks. Unlike the scholar who is above all afraid to be inaccurate, Pritchett is chiefly afraid of being dull. Such an approach runs counter to academic criticism, which attempts to approach literature "scientifically" by papering over the innate subjectivity of criticism with rigorously applied methodologies. What Pritchett does is unique because it depends upon a voracious appetite for reading, a retentive memory, and above all upon sensitivity and a craftsman's understanding of creativity.

In many ways he follows the Renaissance dictum that the function of literature is to instruct and delight. He assumes that novels and stories (he almost never comments on poetry or drama) are written in part to entertain, to please the senses and intellect. He dislikes trivialities, clichés, and pretentiousness in any form. He assumes that an author has something of value to say to readers and that readers of the classics over the centuries have been ordinary people, not critics and professors. One function of literature, then, is to convey truth, and among Pritchett's condemnatory vocabulary are words like *false, contrived, sentimental, bathos,* and *melodrama.* However, he dislikes preaching and rejects the notion that literature is a substitute for religion. "The world is not saved by novelists; and the unreason of the psychological mystics of the twenties seems to us now, I think, a rather shady attempt to get to God by the stage door. . . . I hope we are beginning to see again that egging readers on to personal conversion is not one of the functions of the novel."[8] Nevertheless, he acknowledges that "from the beginning, the English novel set out to protest and teach" (*LN,* 6). He does not formally define "truth" in fiction, but he seems to mean something quite ordinary and commonsensical that one might simply call fidelity to external and internal reality, recognizing that the two are not fixed and may be contradictory. Adherence to surface appearances alone of course is not his primary criterion, though falseness here will lead to censure. Pritchett's definition seems akin to the neoclassicists' emphasis on the generally consistent features of man and society. Thus, many of his essays discuss the continuity between the classics and contemporary life, a relationship he stresses in the preface to *In My Good Books:*

The most satisfying classics at present [1942] are those in which the cries of an age are like echoes of our own. In all the literature of the French Revolution, through the Napoleonic wars to the Reform, we find books which seem to be describing our own times. . . . Everything is there from Bloomsbury of the twenties to the recriminations of the thirties and the fighting of this war. We hold up the crystal sphere; we see ourselves in miniature reflection and, perhaps, if our minds are not too literal, we may also see our future.[9]

Similarly, Pritchett analyzes an author's ability to create "believable" characters and to delve convincingly into their psychology and motivation. His touchstone is frequently Dickens, although he recognizes the caricature and sentimentality that too often mar Dickens's creations. *Don Quixote* is another standard of comparison. Among the French he prefers Balzac (especially *La Cousine Bette* and *Le Cousin Pons*), among the Russians Turgenev and the lesser-known Goncharov, and, of the Americans, Henry James. A good illustration is Pritchett's witty and thoughtful essay on *Oblomov*, which he begins by asserting, "The function of the saints is to assuage the wishes of the unconscious, to appeal to that part of a man which is least apparent to himself, and today we must turn away from the heroic, the energetic, expansive and productive characters. Falstaff the coward, Oblomov the sublime sluggard and absentee, seem to me our natural candidates" (*LN,* 396). He goes on to analyze the novel as a piece of propaganda inadvertently turned into art. Like Cervantes, Goncharov began by disliking his character but ended up loving him. Typically, Pritchett finds similarities among character, author, and readers: "After we have read this book we do not hate idleness, escapism, daydreaming: we love Oblomov" (*LN,* 398). He ends by saying, "The great outsize characters in fiction, like Oblomov, are the revenges of the unconscious" (*LN,* 406).

While Pritchett frequently emphasizes the relevance of a book to contemporary readers, he also likes to explore the interactions between an author's heredity and the environmental forces that influenced him. To some extent he is a biographical critic. An essay on Joseph Conrad, for instance, begins with a discussion of a new biography of the author through which Pritchett associates incidents in Conrad's life with events in his novels. These he uses not simply as sources for the novels but as keys to Conrad's art. Always striving for essences, Pritchett regards the elemental facts of the author's experience and psyche as vital to the success and failures of the artist. An extract from his essay on Balzac illustrates the approach:

Balzac is the novelist of our appetites, obsessions and our *idées fixes,* but his great gift is his sense of the complexity of the human situation. He had both perceptions, one supposes, from his peasant origins, for among peasants, as he was fond of saying, the *idée fixe* is easily started; and their sense of circumstance overpowers all other consideration in their lives. (*LN,* 337–38)

Frequently examinations of this type point to the social and hereditary forces that created significant tensions in the author's life and were then transferred to his fiction. This approach is open to question on theoretical and practical grounds. By emphasizing the connections between a writer's life and art and the relevance of literature to contemporary concerns, Pritchett stresses that all fiction belongs to a living tradition of interest to ordinary readers, not merely highbrows and scholars.

Another value of Pritchett's criticism is the insight it affords into the craft of fiction writing. He does not analyze technique at length but offers perceptive comments on those aspects that set the writer in question apart from others. His comments on D. H. Lawrence are typical:

He reintroduced the direct apprehension of experience. He wrote from within—from inside the man, the woman, the tree, the fox, the mine. His people and his scene, whether it is a German road, a Nottingham kitchen or a Mexican village, are no longer fingered with one hand in the manner of naturalistic writers; they are grasped with both hands, with mind and senses. The impersonal novelist, the god with the fountain pen, has gone; the people, the trees, the mines, the fields, the kitchens come physically upon the page. And although Lawrence is the most personal of novelists, and quite as personal as Thackeray or Meredith were, he does not continually obtrude. At his best, he puts the reader instantly in the scene; instead of drawing it up neatly to be considered with all the feeling left out. (*LN,* 184)

If Pritchett has a fault, it is that his technical insights, quickness of mind, familiarity with the material, and depth of perception sometimes makes challenging reading for the ordinary person. His comment on Graham Greene, for example, presumes a highly literate general reader:

In *The Power and the Glory,* Greene succeeds above all the rest. In the other tales, by quickness of cinematic cutting, by turning everything he sees to the advantage of action, he makes circles round our doubts. The preposterous argument of *Brighton Rock* is lost in the excitement of the hunt. But in the Mexican novel no doubts arise. There is no overt resentment. There are no innuendos. There are no theological conundrums. It is actually an advantage that Greene hated Mexico and the tropical rot; he had worked the worst off in a vivid book, *The Lawless Roads*. Except for the portrait of the seedy Mr. Tench, the dentist, at the beginning, and the account of the Catholic family reading their forbidden literature secretly, there is nothing to distract us from the portraits of the whisky-priest and the lieutenant, his pursuer. In this kind of drama, Mr. Greene excels; but here there is meaning, not fear-fantasy; the priest is taken from depth to depth in physical suffering and spiritual humiliation. The climax is reached when he is disowned by his mistress and his child and this long scene is wonderful for the way in which the feeling is manipulated and reversed. (*TB*, 81)

There is a great deal of insight in this densely packed paragraph, but as usual Pritchett asserts his conclusions and judgments without further discussion. This habit is dictated partly by space limitations, but it is also inherent in his approach to literature. His ideas are illuminating, but they do not appear to be the result of careful analysis. Rather, they have the look of intuitive insights, the products of a highly refined literary sensibility. It does not evidently occur to him that readers may have difficulty following this highly allusive chain of reasoning, that their frame of reference may be narrower, their memory hazy, their apprehension less quick. One sometimes wishes that Pritchett would analyze in more detail or illustrate with more quotations.

Given these qualities, it is not surprising that Pritchett's criticism is most effective when the essay is well focused and clearly developed. Thus, the few pages he devotes to Flannery O'Connor (*TB*, 164–69) delve deeply into her art because he closely examines the texts and concentrates on the theme of evil as the distinguishing mark of her stories. Examples are carefully chosen, plots are summarized, and all is related to the overall thesis. The resulting analysis is clear, perceptive, and satisfying. By contrast, the article on Kipling is diffuse and wavering (*LN*, 175–82). Attention is divided between Kipling and J. M. S. Tompkin's study of him, making the article part review, part essay. Sometimes Pritchett can combine the two effectively, but here he tries to cover too many points—Kipling's popularity, politics, techniques of characterization, and vulgarity—and succeeds in giving each only cursory attention. In such a context even his most perceptive comments, such as the observation that "sentimentality—as distinct from sentiment—arises when we impose an idea upon a feeling in order to obscure it" (*LN,* 180), lose much of their force. However, such lapses are rare. The overall quality is astonishingly high, particularly in view of the enormous number of essays he produced. One wishes that there were more reviewers with Pritchett's abilities to grace the literary magazines that remain.

Meredith, Balzac, and Turgenev

George Meredith and English Comedy (1969) was first presented as the Clark Lectures at Trinity College, Cambridge, in 1969. It bears some marks of its origins in both style and content since Pritchett deliberately avoids detailed analyses that would tax a listening audience. It is unique among his critical writings as the only extended work on a specific theme, his other full-length studies being critical biographies of less concentrated focus. Perhaps for this reason the Meredith study highlights the virtues and limitations of Pritchett's criticism. The first chapter attempts to classify English comic novels into three types: the masculine, the feminine, and the mythic. In the first category Pritchett places Fielding, Scott, Jane Austen, and Ivy Compton-Burnett (among others), finding that "animal spirits, horseplay, good health have their parts especially in the *male* comic writing of the masculine school."[10] The feminine school values "privacy, value, imagination and sensibility more than common sense" (17) and includes Peacock, Lear, Carroll, Virginia Woolf, and others. The third category is similar to the feminine and in it he places only Dickens. Having defined these three types, he does not use them as the basis for the rest of the book or even the rest of the chapter. Instead, he begins a new topic, based on the provocative observation that "it is by his power to interpose and use difficulties that a novelist creates something new and perhaps important" (22). He classifies Meredith's own limitations into three categories: Meredith himself, his poetic impulses, and his inclinations toward romance. From this point on Pritchett concentrates on the tension in Meredith's life—his middle-class origins, Welsh ancestry, and German education—relating these to the limitations of the novels. All of this is rather confusing, although these first two chapters have compensating excellences, particularly an aside on England's colonializing architecture and an extended analysis of Meredith's style. Overall, however, their effect is that of two separate and barely related introductions.

The remaining chapters examine Meredith's major novels. Chapter 3 analyzes the structural flaws in *The Ordeal of Richard Feverel* and relates these to Meredith's egotism. Chapter 4 is devoted to *Harry Richmond* but is only tenuously connected with Meredith's supposed tendencies toward romance, while chapter 5 examines *The Egoist* and returns briefly to Meredith's own ego-related problems.

In spite of these structural flaws, J. I. M. Stewart called Pritchett's discussion of Meredith's novels, "far and away the most just and perceptive they have received."[11] Certainly the book contains many excellent passages of analysis. The comments on individual scenes and characters are astute and revealing, and Pritchett's balanced appreciation of Meredith's gifts is infectious. Convincing, too, are his analyses of the novel's failures, and he is provocative in relating these to the larger problems of Victorian fiction. Overall, this is a highly readable, frequently perceptive, yet sometimes frustrating analysis of a novelist who has received comparatively little attention. One would like a more coherent book, in which the three categories of English comedy were organically related to the discussion of Meredith's rightful place in the history of the novel and in which the limitations that Pritchett enumerates were more systematically explored. The suspicion that Pritchett's difficulties in organizing this book are akin to his problems as a novelist is hard to resist.

Pritchett's first full-length critical biography *Balzac* (1973) is not a scholarly book but a highly readable study for a general audience based on available secondary sources. It was a lively and congenial subject, although in re-creating this rambunctious and volatile Frenchman, Pritchett may exercise more poetic license than a strict regard for the facts would allow. In the early chapters on Balzac's childhood and education he is reliable, but as Balzac progresses from unknown scribbler to successful serious novelist, Pritchett increasingly emphasizes the outlandish, spendthrift, and dreamy sides of his subject, gradually turning him into another Walter Pritchett—an incurable visionary and unconscious manipulator of others (particularly women) with no business sense and a tenuous grasp of reality. Pritchett did not invent these characteristics, but he does overemphasize these aspects of Balzac's character. In speaking of Balzac's disastrous investment in a printshop and type foundry, for example, he comments,

For despite his lifelong groans about the burden of his obligation, the real lesson of his failure to him was the opposite of what would occur to the ordinary man who learns prudence in misfortune: he had lost his financial virginity and saw before him in the licentious territory of debt a Promised Land. He was liberated at last. There was nothing to do but to settle to serious writing about the realities of daily life that he knew so painfully well. There, in that Promised Land, increasing his debts year by year, he would gladly work himself to death in the delusion that he was paying them off.[12]

Pritchett develops this premise about the relationship between Balzac's finances and his art, in the process creating a comic figure of almost epic proportions. Pritchett's Balzac knows no artistic, financial, sexual, or social bounds. Discussing Balzac's rise to fame and fortune, Pritchett becomes colorful and animated:

He proclaimed that his tea came from the special garden kept by mandarins only for the Emperor of China. It was picked by virgins at sunrise and they presented it to the Emperor on their knees. A little was sent by caravan to the Tsar of Russia and Balzac had been privileged to have a supply of it through the Ambassador. At Delphine de Girardin's house he boasted that he had given Jules Sandeau a white horse and kept everyone agape by the account of where he had found it. He even turned to Sandeau and asked him if he was satisfied with it. As if he had suddenly been borne out of the real world he would announce that he had secret powers which had told him exactly where Toussaint Louverture had hidden his treasure in the West Indies and was so carried away that he fell to sketching maps to prove it. (115)

The book continues in this vein for pages, entertainingly, sometimes almost riotously. It makes exuberant reading. We chase Balzac breathlessly from castle to chateau, from one aristocratic mistress to another, through rapidly mounting debts, orgies of work, and roller coaster emotions, until we have before us almost a parody of the romantic artist. However, is this Balzac?

The answer, to judge by other accounts, is yes and no. Pritchett emphasizes the extravagant and feckless side of Balzac's character to the exclusion of other qualities, resulting in a less-than-rounded portrait. Balzac could be sober and sensible as well as wild and impractical, and his realism derived from philosophical as well as commercial motives. One aspect of Balzac's education and character that Pritchett neglects is his philosophical and religious reading. As André Maurois shows,[13] Balzac's peculiar combination of romantic fantasy and scientific realism stemmed from wide reading in philosophy, science, and psychology, as well as from character and environment.

Having said all this, we must still credit Pritchett with a vigorous and thoroughly enjoyable study, free of pedantry and equivocation. Pritchett's characters are strong and clearly delineated; his eye for detail and choice quotation is as acute as ever. The critical passages are relatively infrequent, perhaps because Balzac's output was so vast that to begin evaluating it would be to start down a long and complex road. Pritchett does analyze the major works and, in so doing, occasionally assumes too much knowledge by the general reader. With well-known works like *Père Goriot* and *Eugénie Grandet,* generous assumptions are warranted. With lesser-known but important works like *The Ass's Skin,* confusion can result. He also quotes frequently and at length without translating from the French. Although his interpretation of his subject is one-sided, his rapid pace and clear narrative line make the book a joy for the general reader, even if one might on occasion wish for more information or translation from the French. Pritchett's lively text is supported by a profusion of well-chosen and strategically placed illustrations that assist the reader in savoring Balzac's life and age.

The Gentle Barbarian: The Life and Work of Turgenev (1977) resembles *Balzac* in being a critical biography intended for the general reader, but it presents a more sober and balanced view of his subject. Once again Pritchett's concern is to maintain a strong, crisp narrative line and to re-create a character from the available secondary materials. Pursuing these goals, he finds relatively little time for examining the milieu of his central character, but there are fascinating portraits of Turgenev's friends and contemporaries such as Flaubert, George Sand, and the volatile Dostoyevski. The pace is brisk, following Turgenev's life as if he were the protagonist of a strongly plotted novel, from his lonely childhood on an immense estate, through his student days in Germany and France, to his first stirrings of success as a writer, his frustrating love affair with Pauline Viardot, and finally into his mature years as a successful author caught between political opponents both right and left. The narrative moves through vivid scenes and dramatic moments, punctuated with discussions of Turgenev's works, which are handled with the same agility as the biography. The result is an engaging, energetic, and informative account of an important writer and fascinating person, delivered in a style that is authoritative but unstuffy. The liveliness of the novelist's eye and ear is illustrated by the following passage, describing the return of Turgenev's autocratic mother to her estate at Spasskoye:

> What a hissing of marching geese, what a clatter in the rookeries, what barking of dogs when the coach at last arrived at her mansion. Her serf orchestra struck up a tune of welcome as the peremptory mistress got out. What a kneeling to the ground, what a kissing of hands for the privileged servants, what a ringing of bells from room to room as orders were given, what excited trilling from the scores of cage birds on the walls as the short, gypsyish mistress stared at her "subjects" as she called her forty house serfs, to detect who among them had disobeyed her orders and what punishments she would award. The barking of dogs was stopped at once. She could not bear it.[14]

Creating a scene like this requires the imagination of the fiction writer, not the thorough plodding of the scholar. In these qualities Pritchett's book excels, as well as in the quick wit and discerning eye he turns on Turgenev's writing. As in the critical essays, when he applies his intimate knowledge of the writer's craft, Pritchett is most penetrating:

> How naturally he catches the moment between noticing and not noticing. This, one says, is where his art lies; not simply in seeing, but in the waywardness and the timelessness of seeing. Seeing is like light and shadow, playing over what is seen. Things seen are exact yet they flow away or are retrieved: the past and the present mingle in a clear stream. There are two masters of seeing in Russian literature: Tolstoy and Turgenev. Tolstoy sees exactly as if he were an animal or a bird: and what he sees is still and settled for good. He has the pride of his eye. Turgenev is also exact but without that decisive pride: what he sees is already changing. In one of his letters he quotes with admiration an image of Byron's "the music of the face"—the movement from note to note, the disappearance of the thing seen in time as it passes. (61–62)

From the qualities that make Pritchett such a lively and interesting biographer and critic also come the limitations of his approach. Lacking a scholar's attention to conflicting and inconclusive evidence, Pritchett often speaks with certainty about matters that the facts do not wholly resolve. In the early chapters on Turgenev's background and childhood, for example, he writes almost like an omniscient narrator in a novel, boldly ignoring gaps or contradictions in the evidence. The scholar would stop to ponder the data or carefully annotate his speculations, but Pritchett keeps the story moving. Similarly, the scholar would trace the influence of books, ideas, politics, and the general milieu of the time; Pritchett does some background work but his story will not sustain prolonged examination of all these factors. The result is a clear narrative line, but there is also a rootless quality to his Turgenev. We are told that he is deeply Russian without being shown what that means; characters in the stories and novels are compared to contemporary figures or types, but these are not fully developed or explained. Consequently, the reader is sometimes at Pritchett's mercy, having to trust judgments and conclusions for which little evidence is provided. Thus, the reader who wants to know what kind of man Turgenev was and the sort of books he wrote will find the book admirable, but the reader who wants to place Turgenev and his works in the context of his times will find the book somewhat weak. However, all readers will benefit from Pritchett's incisive analyses and evaluations of Turgenev's works, even those who might appreciate more plot summaries and detailed analysis.

Some maintain that Pritchett's fame will ultimately rest on his criticism, but although he has made enormous contributions to the art of the informal literary essay, this seems improbable. Criticism in the last half of this century is too dominated by scholarly methodology to find room for Pritchett's informal erudition. It would be healthy for the discipline if more attention were paid to the traditional man of letters, but this seems unlikely. Moreover, however good or influential Pritchett's criticism is ultimately judged to be, his short stories are the cornerstone of his reputation.

The Autobiography

In spite of Pritchett's considerable achievements in fiction and criticism, his two volumes of autobiography, *A Cab at the Door* (1968) and *Midnight Oil* (1971) have elicited the most lavish praise from reviewers. One has only to read these wise and entertaining volumes to see why the critics were so enthusiastic. *A Cab at the Door* covers the years from Pritchett's birth to age twenty, shortly before he left for Paris. It is a remarkably frank and personal memoir, not in the "kiss and tell" manner that has become the recent standard, but in an engagingly human sense. Pritchett is candid about his family's lower middle-class background and about his growing pains and adolescent absurdities. The reader is certain from the first page onward that this is autobiography as it should be written—honest, open, detailed, without a shred of self-importance or false humility. Above all is the sense that everything he describes is slightly preposterous and outrageous, including the author himself. The evocations of Pritchett's family and relatives, particularly his absurd father, are like character sketches from his short stories. These and the restless movement of Walter Pritchett's flights from suburb to suburb give the book the vitality of life itself. Equally enthralling are Pritchett's portraits of London's various districts and his depictions of Yorkshire and Norfolk. Edwardian England comes alive in its manners, architecture, smells, customs, schools, and people. We are in the world that Pritchett knew as a boy, from its seedy South London suburbs to its starchy Yorkshire villages. The quarrels and tensions of Pritchett's unusual family, centering on Walter's pursuit of Divine Will and financial solvency, are evoked with equal color and conviction. These details, together with Pritchett's revealing portrait of himself as a frustrated yet toughened youth, make the book a pure pleasure to read.

Midnight Oil seems equally frank and colorful, particularly in its re-creation of Pritchett's Paris. He is sufficiently detached about his own youthful follies and conflicts to present them ironically, yet at times touchingly. As we follow the young man's struggles in Paris and, later, in Ireland while he attempts to find himself as a person and as a writer, we are caught up as if in a comic bildungsroman. Again, the cast of characters is as delightful as it is improbable, from his maternal landlady to the pathetic journalist Percy, and finally to the Irish writers he met briefly in Dublin. He never boasts about his successes or whines over his failures. Nor does he castigate fate or changing times. The man who emerges is tolerant, good-humored, and utterly without pretensions.

These two volumes are autobiography as art rather than as history. Characters, setting, and story line are not contrived, but they have the unity and slightly fantastic air of fiction. It is difficult to recall, at times, that we are reading about real people and actual events. Only when we reread or examine carefully do we realize that the artifice is highly selective, that there are large gaps in the factual account, and that the cast of characters is not only small but largely anonymous. As noted in the biographical sketch, Pritchett breaks off his self-portrait in the late thirties, omitting some forty years of his

life. Conspicuously absent are his wife and family, his literary friends
and acquaintances, his travels, his strivings as a novelist, his work
with the Society of Authors and P. E. N. These omissions stem from
a highly developed sense of privacy and a reluctance to offend. Having
spent fifty years in London literary society, Pritchett must have met
at one time or another virtually every figure of consequence in twentieth-century letters. Yet not one of these persons appears. We do not
have to be voyeurs or gossipmongers to wish that Pritchett's account
of himself and his times were more full and comprehensive. He would
undoubtedly have much of value to say about changes in literary life
over the decades. Moreover, the two volumes together really give us
only a portrait of the artist as a young man. The mature Pritchett
reveals only the most superficial information about himself.

Having made these criticisms, we must nevertheless admit that *A
Cab at the Door* and *Midnight Oil* are fascinating books about a captivating gentleman who will probably never be known intimately except to family and close friends. Perhaps that is as it should be, for
too much candor—or apparent candor—can become its own form of
obfuscation and cant. We come away from these books with a profound respect for their author and a desire to know him in person
because the man we have begun to know is captivatingly human. One
this wise and witty about himself and his times must surely have
much to say about the world and its people. Pritchett does. He has
chosen to say it best through his inimitable short stories, which, together with these splendid memoirs, tell us everything essential about
V. S. Pritchett as a man and an artist.

Chapter Seven
Conclusion

The story of V. S. Pritchett's rise from lower middle-class obscurity to Sir Victor Pritchett, Order of the British Empire, Fellow of the Royal Society of Literature, is a fascinating tale in literary self-education. It seems more American than British, with its overtones of Horatio Alger, and indeed Pritchett admits that American editors were often first to give him opportunities to prove himself. In other respects, however, no writer could be more British than Pritchett, and few have been more fiercely individual and independent. His struggles in school, his almost-crippling family life, his years in the leather trade and afterward as a clerk in Paris, and his long years of work in journalism were hurdles that he overcame by sheer effort and determination. He is, surely, as much a self-made author as it is possible to be. He is justifiably proud of his achievements, and he has chronicled them unforgettably in two volumes of autobiography. In spite of these books, and indeed in spite of the biographical survey in this one, Pritchett remains an unknown quantity, the mystery man of modern British letters. It is not merely morbid curiosity that leads us to wish that we knew more about Pritchett the man. It has frequently been noted in these pages that Pritchett's fiction often derives from personal experience, particularly in the early novels and stories. The same might be true for the later stories as well, but the information enabling us to make such connections is unavailable.

One of the desiderata of Pritchett scholarship, therefore, is a genuinely full and accurate biography. Everything we know of Pritchett helps us to understand his fiction and its unique qualities. This is true not only regarding the events of his life but of his intellectual development as well. Remarkably, considering the vast amount Pritchett has published, he has managed to hide most of his personality and his private thoughts. His struggles with religion and sexuality have been repeatedly mentioned in these pages, and their relevance to his fiction is clear. Yet there are so many aspects of Pritchett's life, particularly since World War II, about which we know nothing that we are forced to see each new story as if it were sui generis; we lack the coherent view of the author's life and thought to link them into a cogent pattern. We are like scientists with a large body of facts and no theory to make them intelligible. Given Pritchett's unwillingness to cooperate with biographers or critics, no such definitive study seems possible during his lifetime, but until a full biography of Sir Victor is published, his work will remain to some extent unknown and unknowable, and the full significance of his heroic struggle to become a writer will remain unappreciated. More to the point, his work may continue to suffer from neglect.

The works that most deserve further study and appreciation are, as has been indicated above, the short stories. Interesting as Pritchett's novels are in parts, they do not succeed as wholes. His imagination is essentially that of a storyteller, an illuminator of lives by lightning flashes of insight and sympathy. He lacks the novelist's gift of sustained imagination and the ability to create and maintain a social world in which his characters can move and develop. He has written well in criticism, biography, autobiography, and travel, but these are not genres on which a lasting readership can be built. The short story as Pritchett perfected it and on which he set his unique stamp is the basis for his present and continuing reputation. Fortunately for him, the genre is enjoying a renaissance at present, and one can therefore hope that the time is right for a sustained and serious consideration of Pritchett's work.

As noted in the previous chapters, what sets a Pritchett story apart from the common run is his ability to delineate character. In a brief but pithy essay William Peden observes, "Regardless of subject or setting, character or idea, Pritchett's best stories are *happenings;* they are trips, in a sense comparable to hallucinogenic trips. Something *happens,* revelations realized or unrealized, trivial or of vital importance to the individual even if, like the commercial traveler of 'Sense of Humour,' he himself is unaware of their significance."[1] Pritchett's people often live double lives, as we all do, carefully hiding from the world and themselves some truth or flaw. Pritchett peels away the protective layers that hide this doubleness, or catches the character off guard, or puts him in a situation that causes stress, and with the stress comes a crack in the facade. But he does so with love and sympathy, not with malice and spite. And there is a significant fact about Pritchett's characters. Although all of them are highly individual and real, few impress themselves on our memories as do the characters of, say, Dickens or Maugham. That is because Pritchett's people are ordinary, so much like ourselves or someone we have met, that they impress themselves on the memory less as whole people than as moments of revelation—the preacher sinking into the river, the sailor striding into the rain, the blind man forcing his love to rub dirt and spittle on his eyes, the old man diving defiantly into the cold Atlantic waves. In other words, Pritchett seldom deals in types or "characters" in the popular sense; rather, in each of his best stories he presents a unique individual in his or her own environment. The result is fiction that is vibrant, fresh, and original.

The short story is such a deceptively simple art that the form and its practitioners have received relatively little critical and scholarly attention. Pritchett, whose full stature as a story writer is only now being apprehended, suffers from dual neglect because he has not written a novel of importance. Apart from reviews and a few brief critical essays and paragraphs in books devoted to the history of the story, Pritchett has enjoyed no sustained critical analysis. The bibliographies list not a single article on his stories. What is needed, therefore, is a lively critical examination of individual stories, recurring themes, stylistic devices, and technical strategies. The subtle chemistry of his stories deserves careful reading and close analysis; the precise nature of his contribution to the genre warrants thorough discussion and debate. Claims of unwarranted neglect have often been made on behalf of second-rate authors whose obscurity is well deserved, but there is nothing second-rate about Pritchett's short stories. They will stand comparison with all but the tiny handful of masterpieces the century has produced.

Pritchett's individuality, indeed his uniqueness, make him a difficult author to classify, and literary historians and critics love to categorize and pigeonhole. This book has made some attempt to put Pritchett into his historical context, to see him as a product of the period between the world wars when extraordinary interest in the short story and a plethora of outlets for it created a generation of writers whose forte is the story. Curiously, nearly all of these resemble Pritchett in their working or middle-class backgrounds and lack of university education. Like him, too, they are largely apolitical writers who do not fit comfortably into the categories and coteries that have thus far dominated our view of twentieth-century fiction. The names of Rhys Davies, Sylvia Townsend Warner, H. E. Bates, A. E. Coppard, William Plomer, Elizabeth Bowen, and Fred Urquhart come readily to mind as Pritchett's compatriots. Collectively, they have compiled a natural history of the ordinary British man and woman, quietly and without political fanfare chronicling the emergence of British economic and political democracy in this century. Pritchett and Bates are probably outstanding in this group, each having contributed something inimitable to the short story. Bates appears to have had no imitators, but Pritchett's influence may be detected in the work of Angus Wilson and Muriel Spark, very different from Pritchett in many ways, much like him in their use of humor and in their focus on the quirks of individual behavior. Whatever Pritchett's place in the scheme of twentieth-century literature, his debt to earlier writers like Wells and Bennett needs to be examined and his influence on later writers deserves evaluation.

Meanwhile, there are the stories themselves, at once so simple and accessible, yet so subtle and elusive. They are the life's work of a remarkable and energetic man who has helped his readers understand themselves and their world more fully.

Notes and References

Chapter One

1. *A Cab at the Door* (New York: Random House, 1967), 3–11. Since there is little published information about Pritchett's life, the material in this section relies heavily on the memoirs. Except for direct quotations, material taken from the autobiography will not be cited, and the reader may assume that information in this section derives from *A Cab at the Door,* unless otherwise noted.

2. Ian Sandbrook, Headmaster of Rosedale School, personal letter to the author, 2 May 1985.

3. Valerie Jenkins, "Smoked, Kippered and a Happy Slave," *Evening Standard,* 11 May 1974, 13.

4. Ibid.

5. Sandbrook to author, 25 January 1985.

6. Jenkins, "Smoked," 13.

7. Sandbrook to author, 25 January 1985.

8. "Looking Back at 80," *New York Times Magazine,* 14 December 1980, 110.

9. *Midnight Oil* (New York: Random House, 1972), 5–9; hereafter cited as *MO* followed by page number in parentheses in the text. As in the previous section, the reader may assume that all information derives from this source unless otherwise noted.

10. J. M. Barrie, *When a Man's Single* (London: Hodder & Stoughton, 1913), 125.

11. *Dublin: A Portrait* (New York: Harper & Row, 1967), 3.

12. "Decree Absolute for the Dissolution of Marriage in the High Court of Justice," 9 September 1936.

13. A. D. Peters to V. S. Pritchett, 17 February 1928. Humanities Research Center, University of Texas at Austin. Subsequent references to this collection will be cited in the text and the correspondents referred to by their initials.

14. These figures are derived from correspondence between A. D. Peters and V. S. Pritchett, 1930–1939.

15. V. S. Pritchett to Gerald Brenan, undated. Humanities Research Center, University of Texas at Austin. Subsequent references to this collection will be cited in the text and the correspondents referred to by their initials.

16. William Pounds to author, 9 October 1984.

17. Gerald Brenan, *Personal Record: 1920–1972* (London: Jonathan Cape, 1974), 337–39.

18. Preface, *In My Good Books* (London: Chatto & Windus, 1942), 9.

19. *New Yorker Magazine* to A. D. Peters, 7 January 1953, 13 March 1953, 2 April 1956, 29 December 1960.

20. "Looking Back at 80," 44.

21. Dr. Robert O. Preyer to author, 5 April 1985.

22. *Observer*, 17 June 1984.

Chapter Two

1. V. S. Pritchett, "1939: The Life We Lost," *Sunday Telegraph*, 2 September 1939, 8.

2. *Marching Spain* (London: Ernest Benn, 1928), 48–49; hereafter page references cited in parentheses in the text.

3. Laurie Lee, *As I Walked Out One Midsummer Morning (New York:* Atheneum, 1969), 61.

4. *Clare Drummer* (London: Ernest Benn, 1930), 12; hereafter page references cited in parentheses in the text.

5. V. S. Pritchett to A. D. Peters, 8 June 1932(?) Date can only be estimated by internal evidence.

6. *The Spanish Virgin* (London: Ernest Benn, 1930), 176; hereafter page references cited in parentheses in the text.

Chapter Three

1. *Shirley Sanz* (London: Victor Gollancz, 1932), 15.

2. *Nothing Like Leather* (London: Chatto & Windus, 1935), 410; hereafter page references cited in parentheses in the text.

3. *Nation*, 26 June 1935, 752.

4. *New Statesman and Nation*, 26 January 1935, 109.

5. *Spectator*, 18 January 1935, 95.

6. *Times Literary Supplement*, 31 January 1935, 60.

7. *Dead Man Leading* (London: Chatto & Windus, 1937), 90; hereafter page references cited in parentheses in the text.

8. "Looking Back at 80," 112.

9. E. B. C. Jones, *Spectator*, 9 April 1937, 676.

10. "Jungle Solitude," *Times Literary Supplement*, 3 April 1937, 256.

11. *You Make Your Own Life and Other Stories* (London: Chatto & Windus, 1938), 209; hereafter page references cited in parentheses in the text.

12. V. S. Pritchett to John Lehmann, 27 June 1936. University of Texas at Austin.

13. John J. Stinson, "The English Short Story, 1945–1950," in *The*

English Short Story 1945–1980, ed. Dennis Vannatta (Boston: Twayne, 1985), 10–13.

Chapter Four

1. "The Literary Scene," in *The Pelican Guide to English Literature: The Modern Age,* ed. Boris Ford (Baltimore: Penguin Books, 1961), 92.

2. *It May Never Happen and Other Stories* (London: Chatto & Windus, 1945), 159; hereafter page references cited in parentheses in the text.

3. *Mr. Beluncle* (London: Chatto & Windus, 1951), 189–90; hereafter references to this novel cited in the text as *B* followed by page number.

4. "Mr. Pritchett's Novels," *Times Literary Supplement,* 19 October 1951, 660.

5. Alex Hamilton, "A Decisive Tonnage of Vitality," *London Times,* 14 October 1977.

6. Elizabeth Bowen, "Books in General," *New Statesman and Nation,* 20 October 1951, 439.

Chapter Five

1. *Why Do I Write? An Exchange of Views Between Elizabeth Bowen, Graham Greene, and V. S. Pritchett* (London: Percival Marshall, 1948), 7; hereafter references cited in the text as *W* followed by page number.

2. Orville Prescott, "Books of the Times," *New York Times,* 27 August 1956, 27.

3. *The Sailor, Sense of Humour and Other Stories* (New York: A. A. Knopf, 1956), v.

4. *When My Girl Comes Home* (London: Chatto & Windus, 1961), 16; hereafter page references cited in parentheses in the text.

5. Norah L. Magid, "Review of *Blind Love and Other Stories,*" *Commonweal* 15 (May 1970):277.

6. *Blind Love and Other Stories* (London: Chatto & Windus, 1969), 93; hereafter page references cited in parentheses in the text.

7. *The Camberwell Beauty and Other Stories* (London: Chatto & Windus, 1975), 179; hereafter page references cited in parentheses in the text.

8. Valentine Cunningham, "Great Tipster," *New Statesman and Nation,* 4 October 1974, 1182.

9. Eudora Welty, "A Family of Emotions," *New York Times Book Review,* 25 June 1978, 1.

10. Benjamin DeMott, "Ironic Comedy," *New York Times Book Review,* 18 November 1979, 42.

11. *On The Edge of the Cliff* (London: Chatto & Windus, 1979), 119; hereafter page references cited in parentheses in the text.

12. Valentine Cunningham, "Coping With the Bigger Words," *Times Literary Supplement,* 25 June 1982, 687.

Chapter Six

1. *The Spanish Temper* (London: Chatto & Windus, 1954), vii; hereafter page references cited in parentheses in the text.

2. Honor Tracy, "Review of *The Spanish Temper,*" *New Statesman and Nation,* 1 May 1954, 567.

3. *London Perceived* (London: Chatto & Windus, 1962), 73–74; hereafter page references cited in parentheses in the text.

4. *New York Proclaimed* (London: Chatto & Windus, 1965), 9; hereafter page references cited in parentheses in the text.

5. *Dublin: A Portrait* (New York: Harper & Row, 1967), 42; hereafter page references cited in parentheses in the text.

6. *The Offensive Traveller* (New York: A. A. Knopf, 1964), 4.

7. *The Tale Bearers* (London: Chatto & Windus, 1980), 87; hereafter references cited in the text as *TB* followed by page number.

8. *The Living Novel and Later Appreciations* (New York: Random House, 1964), 407; hereafter references cited in the text as *LN* followed by page number.

9. *In My Good Books* (London: Chatto & Windus, 1942), 12.

10. *George Meredith and English Comedy* (London: Chatto & Windus, 1969), 15; hereafter page references cited in parentheses in the text.

11. J. I. M. Stewart, "Master of Contrivance," *New Statesman and Nation,* 8 May 1970, 664.

12. *Balzac* (London: Chatto & Windus, 1973), 79; hereafter page references cited in parentheses in the text.

13. André Maurois, *Prometheus: The Life of Balzac,* trans. Norton Denny (New York: Harper & Row, 1965).

14. *The Gentle Barbarian: The Life and Work of Turgenev* (London: Chatto & Windus, 1977), 4–5; hereafter page references cited in parentheses in the text.

Chapter Seven

1. "V. S. Pritchett," in *The English Short Story, 1880–1945,* ed. Joseph M. Flora (Boston: Twayne, 1985), 150.

Selected Bibliography

PRIMARY SOURCES

1. Short Stories

Blind Love and Other Stories. London: Chatto & Windus, 1969; New York: Random House, 1969.

The Camberwell Beauty and Other Stories. London: Chatto & Windus, 1974; New York: Random House, 1974.

Collected Stories. London: Chatto & Windus, 1956. Republished as *The Sailor, Sense of Humour, and Other Stories.* New York: A. A. Knopf, 1956.

Collected Stories. London: Chatto & Windus, 1982; New York: Random House, 1982.

It May Never Happen and Other Stories. London: Chatto & Windus, 1945; New York: Reynal, 1947.

The Key to My Heart. London: Chatto & Windus, 1963; New York: Random House, 1964.

More Collected Stories. London: Chatto & Windus, 1983; New York: Random House, 1983.

On the Edge of the Cliff and Other Stories. London: Chatto & Windus, 1979; New York: Random House, 1979.

The Saint and Other Stories. Harmondsworth, U. K.: Penguin, 1966.

Selected Stories. New York: Random House, 1978.

The Spanish Virgin and Other Stories. London: Ernest Benn, 1930.

When My Girl Comes Home. London: Chatto & Windus, 1961; New York: A. A. Knopf, 1961.

You Make Your Own Life. London: Chatto & Windus, 1938.

2. Novels

Clare Drummer. London: Ernest Benn, 1929.

Dead Man Leading. London: Chatto & Windus, 1937; New York: Macmillan, 1937. Reprint. New York: Oxford University Press, 1985.

Mr. Beluncle. London: Chatto & Windus, 1951; New York: Harcourt, Brace & Co., 1951.

Nothing Like Leather. London: Chatto & Windus, 1935; New York: Macmillan, 1935.

Shirley Sanz. London: Victor Gollancz, 1932. Republished as *Elopement into Exile.* Boston: Little, Brown, 1932.

3. Criticism

Balzac. London: Chatto & Windus, 1973; New York: A. A. Knopf, 1973.

Books in General. London: Chatto & Windus, 1953; New York: Harcourt, Brace, 1953. Reprint. Westport, Conn.: Greenwood Press, 1970.

The Gentle Barbarian: The Life and Work of Turgenev. London: Chatto & Windus, 1977; New York: Random House, 1977.

George Meredith and English Comedy: The Clark Lectures for 1969. London: Chatto & Windus, 1970; New York: Random House, 1970.

In My Good Books. London: Chatto & Windus, 1942. Reprint. Port Washington, N.Y.: Kennicat Press, 1970.

The Living Novel. London: Chatto & Windus, 1946. Revised edition, *The Living Novel and Other Appreciations.* New York: Random House, 1964.

A Man of Letters. London: Chatto & Windus, 1985; New York: Random House, 1986.

The Myth Makers: Literary Essays. London: Chatto & Windus, 1979; New York: Random House, 1979.

Shakespeare: The Comprehensive Soul. London: British Broadcasting Corporation, 1965.

The Tale Bearers: Literary Essays. London: Chatto & Windus, 1980; New York: Random House, 1980.

Why Do I Write? (with Elizabeth Bowen and Graham Greene). London: Marshall, 1948.

The Working Novelist. London: Chatto & Windus, 1965; New York: Random House, 1965.

4. Travel

Dublin: A Portrait. London: Bodley Head, 1967; New York: Harper & Row, 1967.

Foreign Faces. London: Chatto & Windus, 1964. Republished as *The Offensive Traveller.* New York: A. A. Knopf, 1964.

London Perceived. London: Chatto & Windus, 1962; New York: Harcourt, Brace & World, 1962.

Marching Spain. London: Ernest Benn, 1928.

New York Proclaimed. London: Chatto & Windus, 1965; New York: Harcourt, Brace & World, 1965.

The Other Side of the Frontier: A V. S. Pritchett Reader. London: Robin Clark, 1984.

The Spanish Temper. London: Chatto & Windus, 1954; New York: A. A. Knopf, 1955.

5. Autobiography

"As Old as the Century." *Observer,* 14 December 1980, 23, 25. Republished as "Looking Back at 80." *New York Times Magazine,* 14 December 1980, 40 + .

A Cab at the Door. London: Chatto & Windus, 1968; New York: Random House, 1968.

Midnight Oil. London: Chatto & Windus, 1971; New York: Random House, 1972.
The Turn of the Years. Wilton, U. K.: Michael Russell, 1981. Pritchett's essay "As Old as the Century" with engravings by Reynolds Stone and an introduction by Paul Theroux.

6. Edited Works
The Oxford Book of Short Stories. New York: Oxford University Press, 1981.
Robert Louis Stevenson, Novels and Stories. London: Pilot Press, 1945; New York; Duell, 1946.
This England. London: New Statesman & Nation, 1937.
Turnstile One: A Literary Miscellany from The New Statesman and Nation. London: Turnstile Press, 1948.

7. Uncollected Stories
"Agranti, for Lisbon." *Fortnightly Review,* August 1930, 235–46.
"The Ape Who Lost His Tail." *New Writing,* n.s. 1 (Autumn 1938):233–40.
"The Chimney." *New Statesman and Nation,* 26 December 1936, 1061–63.
"Cup Final." *New Statesman and Nation,* 18 December 1943, 398–99.
"Doctor's Story." *New Statesman and Nation,* 3 January 1948, 8–9.
"The Educated Girl." *Transatlantic Review,* no. 5 (December 1960):51–56.
"Goldfish." *New Statesman and Nation,* 26 December 1942, 422–23.
"Hiawatha Complex." *New Statesman and Nation,* 29 December 1956, 835–36.
"I Passed By Your Window." *London Mercury,* December 1938, 131–44.
"In Autumn Quietly." *John o' London's Weekly,* 4 February 1933, 713–15.
"The Invader." *New Statesman and Nation,* 11 January 1941, 34–35.
"Jury." *Fortnightly Review,* March 1937, 321–27.
"Neighbors." *New Yorker,* 5 July 1982, 28–37.
"New World." *John o' London's Weekly,* 22 December 1939, 373–74.
"A Public Benefactress." *Bystander,* 17 August 1938, 265 + .
"Serious Question." *Fortnightly Review,* February 1931, 209–17.
"Slooter's Vengeance." *New Statesman and Nation,* 28 March 1931, vi–vii.
"Trip to the Seaside." *Atlantic Monthly,* 247 (February 1981): 58–64.
"The Truth About Mrs. Brown." *Nash's Pall Mall,* March 1936, 111–27.
"Uncle for Christmas." *News Chronicle,* 12 April 1939.
"Upstairs, Downstairs." *Night and Day,* 1 July 1937.
"Woolly Gloves." *Fortnightly Review,* June 1931, 804–16.

SECONDARY SOURCES

Allen, **Walter.** "V. S. Pritchett." In *Contemporary Novelists,* 1118–21. 2d ed. New York: St. Martin's Press, 1976. Analyzes Pritchett's interest in puritanism and provides a good discussion of *Nothing Like Leather.*

————. "V. S. Pritchett." In *The Short Story in English,* 268–75. New York: Oxford University Press, 1981. Calls Pritchett the best British short story writer since D. H. Lawrence and an author of great originality. Allen emphasizes Pritchett's understanding of the puritan and notes the widening scope of his interest in the later stories. Among the best essays on Pritchett's short stories.

Borkland, Elmer, ed. "V. S. Pritchett." In *Contemporary Literary Critics,* 422–28. New York: St. Martin's Press, 1977. A balanced evaluation of Pritchett's criticism with a valuable discussion of his critical principles.

Bowen, Elizabeth. "Books in General." *New Statesman and Nation,* 20 October 1951, 718–19. A review of *Mr. Beluncle* that laments the "smallness" of most contemporary novels and analyzes Beluncle's character. Her conclusion that *"Mr. Beluncle* not only reasserts but enriches the English novel tradition," overstates the case, but many other comments are astute.

Crews, Frederick C. "Review of *The Key to My Heart.*" *New York Review of Books,* 3 December 1964, 5. Finds the book delightful but forgettable because the society it describes and the concerns it raises are out of fashion.

Cunningham, Valentine. "Coping With the Bigger Words." *Times Literary Supplement,* 25 June 1982, 687. A perceptive review of *Collected Stories* with an especially astute analysis of Pritchett's style and themes. Particular attention is given to "Many Are Disapppointed" and what the reviewer calls Pritchett's "heroicisms of banal life."

————. "Great Tipster." *New Statesman and Nation,* 4 October 1974, 1182. Finds the contemporary short story preferable to the novel and Pritchett's stories in *The Camberwell Beauty* appealing for their characters and sense of place. Also notes a pattern of phallic symbolism in the collection.

————. "The Reader on the Scent." *Times Literary Supplement,* 26 September 1980, 1070. Highly praises *The Tale Bearers* for its understanding of an author's methods, commitment to literature, and engagement with life and language.

DeMott, Benjamin. "Ironic Comedy." *New York Times Book Review,* 18 November 1979, 1, 41–42. A very positive review of *On the Edge of the Cliff,* containing excellent analyses of the title story and "The Accompanist."

The English Short Story 1945–1980. Edited by Dennis Vannatta. Boston: Twayne, 1985. Pritchett's contribution to the short story since 1945 is briefly discussed by three authors who contributed to this collaborative history of the modern English story. A reliable guide to Pritchett and his contemporaries, with several excellent analyses of individual stories.

Field, Louise Maunsell. "A Strong and Fine Tale of a Jungle Journey."

New York Times, 12 September 1937, 3, 27. The longest and most balanced review of *Dead Man Leading,* generally favorable but critical of the book's "overmeticulous" psychology.

Hamilton, Alex. "A Decisive Tonnage of Vitality." *London Times,* 14 October 1971. Part review of *Midnight Oil,* part interview with Pritchett, valuable for Pritchett's comments on himself and his work.

Hayes, Richard. "The Private Necessity." *Commonweal,* 11 September 1953, 564–66. An insightful if rather metaphorical appreciation of *Books in General,* praising the "masculine grace" of Pritchett's prose and the "feminine openness" of his sensibility.

Jenkins, Valerie. "Smoked, Kippered and a Happy Slave." *Evening Standard,* 11 May 1974, 13. A lively article in which the reporter returns with Pritchett to his home in Dulwich and uncovers details omitted from *A Cab at the Door.* An excellent short biography/interview.

Kermode, Frank. "Books in General." *New Statesman and Nation,* 19 March 1965, 455–56. Kermode praises Pritchett's lack of methodology and his understanding of the way a novelist creates.

"The Land of Spain." *Times Literary Supplement,* 23 April 1954, 262. Though objecting that *The Spanish Temper* is not well organized, the reviewer places Pritchett's book in the small circle of outstanding works about Spain. A judicious appraisal.

Lewis, Peter. "Loner With a Master's Touch." *Daily Telegraph,* 14 December 1980, 21. Biographical sketch and interview on Pritchett's eightieth birthday, particularly interesting for Pritchett's description of his writing methods.

Liebling, A. J. "Perception Perceived." *New Yorker,* 9 February 1963, 131–35. A detailed summary of *London Perceived* with a few enthusiastic remarks about the book's text and photographs.

Marcus, Stephen. "An Ideal Critic." *New York Review of Books,* 8 October 1964, 12–15. The best analysis of Pritchett's strengths and weaknesses as a critic, noting his perception and sensitivity but also his inattention to many of the outstanding writers of the twentieth century.

Marks, Harry S. "V. S. Pritchett." In *Dictionary of Literary Biography,* vol. 15, pt. 2, 464–71. Detroit: Gale Research, 1983. A biographical sketch and overview of Pritchett's work, fiction and nonfiction, but with emphasis on the novels. The concise plot summaries and incisive criticisms of the novels are excellent, but his discussion of the short stories is brief. A good, reliable introduction to Pritchett and his accomplishments.

Maxwell, William. "The Two Merlins." *New Yorker,* 29 August 1970, 77–78. In this review of *George Meredith and English Comedy* Pritchett is hailed as a brilliant critic and the book as "a shining example of what" literary criticism can be."

"Mr. Pritchett's Novels." *Times Literary Supplement,* 19 October 1951, 660. Partly a review of *Mr. Beluncle* and partly an appraisal of Pritchett's accomplishments in fiction to that time. The contrast between the structural uncertainties of the novels and the firmness of the better short stories is particularly illuminating.

Muchnic, Helen. "The Wayward Vision." *Saturday Review,* 14 May 1977, 22–25. This excellent review of *The Gentle Barbarian* emphasizes Pritchett's ability to make historical people come alive and his astuteness as a critic in understanding the qualities of Turgenev's fiction.

Nichols, Lewis. "Talk With V. S. Pritchett." *New York Times Book Review,* 25 April 1954, 16. A brief discussion of *The Spanish Temper* and an interview with Pritchett that provides some details about his life and working methods.

O'Brien, Conor Cruise. "In Quest of Uncle Tom." *New York Review of Books,* 14 September 1967, 10–11. Finds the tone of Pritchett's *Dublin: A Portrait* gentle and his account of Irish history biased in favor of moderate Sinn Feiners.

Peden, William. *"Blind Love and Other Stories." Saturday Review,* 14 March 1970, 39–40. An enthusiastic review of *Blind Love* with very useful comments on the dualities of Pritchett's characters and the dramatic nature of his stories. Also contains a brief interview with Pritchett.

———. "V. S. Pritchett." In *The English Short Story 1880–1945,* 143–51. Boston: Twayne, 1985. Peden describes a Pritchett story as a "happening" and provides brief, incisive comments on many of Pritchett's best stories. The essay also includes Pritchett's comments on his own work, derived from Peden's interview with him. An excellent analysis and critique.

Plomer, William. "The Charm of Rats." *London Mercury,* March 1938, 549–50. Reviewing *You Make Your Own Life,* Plomer observes that Pritchett reaches essential truths by paying close attention to surfaces. He also appreciates Pritchett's abilities to portray character and understand the "laws" of human behavior.

Prescott, Orville. "Books of the Times." *New York Times,* 29 August 1956, 27. Ambivalent, generally negative review of *The Sailor, Sense of Humour and Other Stories,* criticizing Pritchett for "coldly analytical compassion."

"Pritchett, V(ictor) S(awdon)." *Current Biography,* 1974, 327–30. A good biographical sketch together with some incisive remarks on Pritchett's works in all genres.

Quennell, Peter. "New Novels." *New Statesman and Nation,* 26 January 1935, 109. A highly positive review of *Nothing Like Leather,* with a good analysis of Matthew Burkle.

Reid, B. L. "Putting the Self In." *Sewanee Review* 85 (Spring 1977):262–85. Part summary, part review of *Midnight Oil,* this extended essay is sensitive to Pritchett's achievement but also laments his diffidence and reticence.

Solotaroff, Theodore. "Autobiography as Art." In *The Red Hot Vacuum and Other Pieces on the Writing of the Sixties,* 284–90. New York: Atheneum, 1970. A review of *A Cab at the Door,* stressing the differences in tone and method between Pritchett and other current autobiographers. Solotaroff prefers Pritchett's artistic approach to excessive candor, praising Pritchett for his honesty and luminous writing.

Strong, L. A. G. "Review of *Shirley Sanz.*" *Spectator,* 6 February 1932, 189. An evenhanded but generally favorable assessment that praises Pritchett's characterizations and ability to dramatize.

Vannatta, Dennis. "V. S. Pritchett." In *Critical Survey of Short Fiction,* vol. 6, 2128–33. Englewood Cliffs, N.J.: Salem Press, 1981. A thoughtful essay on Pritchett's short stories, emphasizing his unusual characters, wit, and sympathy. Vannatta sees Pritchett as a humorist with compassion for those he portrays.

Vidal, Gore. "Secrets of the Shell." *New York Review of Books,* 28 June 1979, 6–7. Vidal enthusiastically endorses *The Myth Makers,* contrasting Pritchett favorably with academic critics, praising his ability to describe, assimilate, and evaluate what he has read. An intelligent appreciation of Pritchett's skill as a critic.

Welty, Eudora. "A Family of Emotions." *New York Times Book Review,* 25 June 1978, 1, 39–40. A joyous review of *Selected Stories,* praising Pritchett's characters and the intensity of his writing, particularly his ability to "fuse" conflicting emotions within a character. Good analyses of several stories.

Index